WHAT IS LOVE?

Awakening the Truth for Healthy Relationships

Exposition, Journal and Workbook

O'Neal

Front cover photo by Shelby Deeter

Copyright © 2019 by BJ O'Neal, Jr.

All rights reserved. No part of this book may be reproduced or transmitted in any form or by any means, electronic or mechanical, including photocopying, recording or by any information storage and retrieval system, without the permission in writing from the copyright owner.

ISBN: 9781798433287

This book was printed in the United States of America.

Scripture quotations taken from the Amplified® Bible (AMP),
Copyright © 2015 by The Lockman Foundation
Used by permission. www.Lockman.org

CONTENTS

Message from the Author 5

What is Love 6

What is Love 7

Love is Patient 13

Love is Kind 20

Love Does Not Envy 28

It Does Not Boast 37

Love is not Proud 44

Love is not Rude 50

Love is not Self-Seeking 59

Love is not Easily Angered 68

It Keeps No Record of Wrongs 74

Love Does Not Delight in Evil, But Rejoices with the Truth 85

Love Always Protects 96

Love Always Trusts 110

Love Always Hopes 120

Love Always Perseveres 130

Love Never Fails 139

Dedication:

To Philip and Valenceia for being friends that love and support like family, and for wrapping your care and love around us. I believe in your union.

Message from the Author

After I published the book, *What is Love?: Awakening the Truth for Healthy Relationships,* some friends of mine suggested that I also create a workbook to go along with it. I have read many books along with their available workbooks. These were great experiences. I was able to affirm what I had learned from the material. Often, many of them also included prayers and requested that I connect the material to my personal life. I believe that is the essential role of a workbook. I understood why they wanted me to create the workbook.

However, as I considered the possibilities, I wanted this workbook to offer the reader a little more. To discover healthier relationships, I want to make sure that you do the work in your relationship. I want to make sure you work on yourself. Those were key ingredients for taking my marriage to new levels. For that reason, I decided to forgo the typical application of rewriting what you just read. Again, the process does offer great value; however, if you want to highlight the material in the book, I suggest highlighting inside the book and creating your own personal journal for those purposes.

In setting the stage for you to do the activities, it turns out that I essentially wrote a whole new book of material. There are so many newly offered reference points, perspectives and insights in this workbook. I provided more examples and more information. As I move forward, I am gaining further insight and have connected it to so many other experiences in my own life. I have included them as a bonus in this workbook.

Lastly, what I want to emphasize is that a workbook has no power if you do not commit to doing the work requested of you. I hope you will go further than simply answering the questions within this workbook. Engage in the conversations, evaluate your works and actions, and commit to making your heart and your relationship healthier than it has ever been before. You can do all the activities with your significant other, but not all of them require it. Some of us are in seasons where we have to seemingly work on our relationships on our own. Believe me when I say that you can make a difference all by yourself. I believe, if you put a genuine effort in place and the resilience to press through, you will see a side of yourself that you have never witnessed before, and you will witness God transform the DNA of your relationship. I hope you will be more than excited about your journey.

Sincerely,

BJ O'Neal, Jr.

Introduction:

What is Love

Introduction

What is Love

When my wife, Stephanie, and I were in the dating phase of our relationship, among other appreciative events, we took the time to tell each other about our major faults: things we were ashamed of and even habits that we assumed may be embarrassing if people ever knew about them. For us, it was an opportunity to accept "the worst" of each other up front, at least the worst that we were familiar with.

These conversations did offer some value and sense of security; however, looking back, it is interesting that we talked about these things but never talked about what love meant to each other. I suppose we thought we were just living it out or that, because there was so much great energy between us, love must have been understood. If we were thinking that way, at that time, we were very far from the truth.

What is interesting is that, for those of us who desire companionship, we play out what we envision love looking like in our minds, but we rarely communicate that picture to the people we are interested in. When what we are experiencing contradicts what we envision in our minds, we get disappointed and even criticize our significant others for not living up to an expectation we never communicated. Most of the time, we don't communicate it because we have never really taken out the time to process what it means to us; we only see what it looks like to us.

Write out the definition of love that has guided your actions and perspective within your relationship experiences.

_____
_____
_____
_____
_____
_____
_____

Introduction

What are some ways you've attempted to demonstrate love? In your opinion, how effective were those methods?

_____
_____
_____
_____
_____
_____
_____
_____
_____
_____

What are some effective ways that people have communicated love to you? How did you know love was fueling their actions?

_____
_____
_____
_____
_____
_____
_____
_____
_____

One of the main reasons modern day love is perverted is that we pursue others with wrong or selfish motives, so we reap the bad fruit of those motives. Take a moment and recall any bad fruit or bad results you have reaped from wrong motives in your relationships?

_____

_____

_____

_____

_____

_____

_____

_____

_____

_____

_____

Activity
Sit down with your significant other or someone who's opinion you value and exchange your ideas of love. Prepare for healthy rebuttals or questions?

Read and meditate on I Corinthians 13:1-3, Matthew 22:36-40, and I John 4:7-8.
How important has understanding and operating in love been to you in the past? After reading the scriptures, where do you believe God has set the priority of love? Have you been on the same page with God in this regard? What actions can you take and what mindset can you take on to further align your priority of love with God's? Meditate on these questions and have a sincere, honest conversation with yourself and answer these questions.

_____

_____

Introduction

First Things First

In the scriptures, Jesus informs us that the second greatest commandment is to love our neighbor as we love ourselves. In recent times, there has been a discovery that states that we must learn how to love ourselves to be able to love our neighbors, and this is true. We need to love ourselves. Before I get into what that looks like, I want to remind us that this was the second greatest commandment and not the first. The first great commandment was to love God with all our hearts and all our minds.

Both, in the New Testament and the Old, God informs us that, if we are to love Him, we are to obey His commandments. So, yes, we need to learn to love ourselves better, but not at the omission or at a priority over learning to love God. The Self Love Movement has been built upon taking time to take care of self, addressing areas of our lives we may have put off or neglected due to lack of esteem or from the pressures to prioritize other things such as our jobs and other responsibilities.

The people who have taken upon the self-love initiative have devoted a great amount of time and energy towards this pursuit, but have we been as tenacious in our pursuit to demonstrate and act upon our love for God? Is God, too, being neglected or becoming second rate to us pursuing our own desires? Maybe or maybe not. I do know of some people who are intentionally desiring to get closer to God as a benefit to self. I would think that God desires that we get closer to Him. Here is an honest question we must ask ourselves, though: when "self-love" contradicts or conflicts with an act of love towards God, which initiative has priority in our hearts?

I've seen people neglect spouses and perhaps children in efforts to take care of self. You may not receive this as neglecting God, but His command is to serve Him by serving others, especially our spouses and children. This doesn't mean giving them everything they desire, but it does mean supplying them with their genuine needs that we are responsible for providing. However, I have heard a loud voice from the crowd saying, "I am not in a place to focus on these things, right now." I would like to offer a very honest response to that voice: we may not function in perfection in this area, but by being obedient to God in this area, He will offer the grace for growth and the wisdom to accomplish what we can if we are seeking Him in this area. Men, the sole focus on self is like working hard on a job, earning a sizable wage, yet our families are living in poverty, lacking food, a home and clothing. Women, the sole focus on self is like building a stable and clean home life, full of safety and security, yet your family is on the street living in chaos and confusion. The bottom line is that we cannot neglect each other in the process of taking care of self. We must find a healthy balance.

If you feel like you are lacking due to your mate's drive to focus on self, do not be discouraged. Many of us mean well in this pursuit. Offer them patience and understanding. Celebrate what they have accomplished in this pursuit. Partner with them with their personal goals. You will indirectly achieve drawing the two of you together, anyway. After all, most of if not all of what they are aspiring for will be something you desire for them as well.

The overall danger of focusing on self before God is that too much emphasis on self will conflict with our devotion towards God. When it comes time to, in the name of God, sacrifice part of this image and identity we have created for ourselves to fulfill His desires, if we have built up ourselves in priority over our love for Him, we will choose ourselves. When the rich man approached Jesus and asked what more he needed to do

Introduction

to inherit the kingdom of God, he stated he had followed so many of God's commandments. Jesus looked at him and examined his heart and requested that he sell all his possessions and give it to the poor. The rich man had devoted much to his wealth and had deeply valued it, even above inheriting the kingdom of heaven. Discouraged, he turned and went his way. Be careful not to place so much value on building an area of your life up so much to the point it conflicts with your capacity to experience the kingdom of heaven. I believe, in the pursuit of self-love, building ourselves up spiritually is the most rewarding focus and initiative we can pursue. In that pursuit, God will not lead us to neglect those things that matter the most to Him. Those things that we personally need and desire will be there for us as well. He promised that if we would seek after Him and all His righteousness that all these things would be added unto us – all the things that we need.

You are worth the love, because God has called you His own. No one can love you better than Him, not even you. Learn to love Him first, and He will teach you how to love yourself and others. God has invested a lot of Himself in love so much that He has allowed it to define Him. If you want to master love on any level: loving God, self, your mate, your children, friends or enemies, God's commandments are the essential principles upon which to build your maturity in these areas. One thing about love is that it never desires to harm the one who receives the love. Do not harm yourself by pursuing other initiatives that separate you from God and those things He desires you to steward in your life. Remember the principle, love God, He will reveal how to love self as we shape your identity through Him, and He will enable you to love others as He reveals just how He has displayed His love towards you.

Declaration

God, I want to learn how to love You with all my heart. I trust You with my life and believe Your greatest desire for me is for my good. I call on Your spirit to guide me along the way. I believe Your grace will cover me along the way. I do not have to be perfect, but I will be convinced that Your ways are beyond and more effective than my ways in pursuing the desires within my heart. I will rely on Your abundant love for me to define my affirmation and self-love. I will acknowledge the greatness of Your love for me and extend it to others, especially towards those I am in relationship with. I acknowledge there is a difference between how You and the world view and pursue love. I choose Your way. The world's way leads to destruction and disappointment. Your way leads to all Your promises. I will become disciplined in following your principles and commandments. I will see the fruit of my obedience. Through my relationship with You, all my other relationships will flourish. You will purge the bad, restore the broken, renew our faith and add favor to our situations. I believe it and declare it in Jesus' name. Amen.

Chapter 1:

Love is Patient

Chapter 1
LOVE IS PATIENT

Traditionally, I'd like to think of myself as a patient guy. I mean I can wait and wait and wait and not show the least sign of distress. Have you ever put someone on hold, had a long conversation on the other line and then finally hung up just to hear your phone ring back because the person on hold never hung up the phone? Well, I've been that person that was put on hold. Even though I was good at waiting, after studying what being patient is I realized that this was not necessarily an indication that I had actual patience.

Now, after committing so many blows to my marriage at the onset, I really wanted to be a different husband. I wanted the relationship to work, so I then committed to growing and offering my wife something so much better. However, just because I was now trying to do things the right way, it didn't mean that all my wife's trust and admiration in me would just instantly return. I had to be understanding that it would be a process – a process that I couldn't dictate nor control when we would "arrive" at a new, desirable place in our marriage. There would be upsets and disappointments along the way that would honestly cause me a lot of hurt. While I tried to be this new guy, her energy and attitude would still be addressing the old guy, and that can be annoying. Even though I knew better than to attack her during these times, something that should be addressed was my heartfelt attitude towards the situation. Was I resentful towards her, though I dare not say? Was I understanding and still believing that a great marriage was still on the way? These deeper characteristics would determine whether the signature of patience was in my character and actions.

A common prayer that people make is "God, help me to be more patient." Some people will readily advise people to be aware of this prayer because it is known that God does not magically zap us with supernatural patience, but He will give us opportunities to work on being patient.

What areas of your life and in your relationships do you believe you struggle with patience the most?

_____
_____
_____
_____
_____

Why do you believe you lack patience in these areas?

_____
_____
_____
_____
_____
_____
_____

      I don't think anyone in the history of mankind ever said that waiting on something or someone is the most exciting thing alive… or maybe someone has said it. Imagine a child on Christmas Eve. Year after year, his parents spend the night putting the final touches on wrapping his gifts. He knows that when he wakes up the next day, he will have the opportunity to see what cool gifts they bought him. He's been waiting since they put the tree up the day after Thanksgiving. Along with all the important stories of Christmas, that tree meant one personal special thing to him: gifts! While he waited throughout the month, he recalls all the subtle hints at the things he said he really wanted that year. While he waited, he envisioned himself sharing his new gifts with his friends, spending hours a week on that new video game, and looking at stars with that new telescope his parents hinted that he may be getting. He is so excited because he understands that the inevitable is that he will be sitting under the tree soon, opening the heartfelt gifts from his parents.

      In this chapter, we acknowledged that patience is waiting with triumphant joy. This child does not mind waiting because he keeps the joy of what he is anticipating at the forefront of his mind.

      In all honesty, one advantage that this child has that we are not always privileged to is that he knew when his desire would be fulfilled – on Christmas Day. For most of us, the reason operating in patience is a challenge is because one of the *who, what, why* or *how* questions are denied a specific answer. Without an answer, we lack control over the situation, so our confidence, comfortability and security are all challenged. Desiring to control the intricate form within any situation will challenge operating with patience. You've been wanting him to fix the sink, but he hasn't done so yet. She will not drive a mile over the speed limit, but you fear you won't make it to the event on time. You've been praying to God to fix a certain area of your relationship, but you are still dealing with the problems in that area.

Chapter 1

Lose Control
What area of your life or relationship is met with impatience due to unmet expectations or due to a lack of control over the situation?

_____
_____
_____
_____
_____
_____
_____

When we operate outside of patience, we choose efforts to control or manipulate our situations to achieve our desires. We offer bargains. If you will fix the sink this weekend, I'll cook your favorite dish. We try to take over. Let me drive so if we get pulled over, at least, I'll get the ticket. We offer ourselves supplements. I decide to talk to a friend on the phone more periodically because she seems to support me in this area more than my wife does.

Honesty Call
When have you tried to manipulate or rush a process to get what you wanted out of your relationship?

_____
_____
_____
_____
_____
_____
_____

LOVE IS PATIENT

If you were building a new home, you wouldn't want the contractor to take shortcuts to build the house quicker. You would not feel safe in the house. You would be unsure that the house could sustain the elements of weather and endure the normal wear and tear. The same applies to the car you drive. If something had malfunctioned, you wouldn't want the mechanic to do a rush job. You may appreciate a timely job so that you can get back to your regular life, but not at the expense of not feeling safe driving in your vehicle.

In this chapter, we discussed that patience isn't merely waiting; it is waiting in the presence of annoyances and/or agitation. We lack patience when we put too much attention and energy on the annoyances.

When we are operating in impatience, we are operating with a different mindset than those who are patient. We begin to place more emphasis and concern on when than we do with the desire itself. Patience maintains the joy that it will happen and the confidence that when it happens it will happen in the right way. Like the boy opening his gifts, the family moving into their newly built home and the woman confidently driving in her repaired car, the joy of obtaining the desire was not diminished by the time lapse that was endured to get it.

Impatience will lead us to resent the very thing we desired because we didn't receive it right when we desired it. Have you ever gone to a restaurant and they took a little too long to prepare your meal? Some of us elected to just leave. We had our appetite ready for a dish, but we forfeited that opportunity because the meal wasn't ready when we thought it should have been ready. Because she drove the speed limit the entire way, even though you have arrived at your destination, your ugly attitude about the drive now causes you not to be able to enjoy her and the event. Your husband is finally coming around to working diligently on being a better man, but since it took too long, your resentment wars with his efforts. Patience waits with triumphant joy. Impatience waits with inevitable demise.

What is a situation where impatience got the best of you? What was the outcome?

_____

_____

_____

_____

_____

Chapter 1

_____

_____

When was a time you exercised patience? What was your reward for your patience?

_____

_____

_____

_____

_____

_____

_____

Not only does patience ensure that we wait for the desire to be prepared in the right way, it is there to ensure that we are also being prepared for the very thing we desire. While what we are desiring is being shaped, the intent is that we are being shaped as well.

And not only this, but [with joy] let us exalt (to show or feel a lively or triumphant joy) in our sufferings and rejoice in our hardships, knowing that our hardship (distress, pressure, trouble) produces patient endurance; and endurance, proven character (spiritual maturity); and proven character, hope and confident assurance [of eternal salvation]. ~ Romans 5:3-4

Patience is a pathway for spiritual maturity. While the contractor is building homes, God is building us. As the scripture indicates, our character, hope and assurance comes through patient endurance. It is a discipline to keep our values at the forefront of our minds despite annoyances and torments. Impatience resolves us to act out of our flesh. We become short and rude in language. We insult and tear down. We disconnect from those we profess to love and have compassion for. Understand that having patience isn't solely important to ensure we can be loving to people we care about; it is necessary to allow God to build us because He cares about us.

Practical Application

In this chapter, we discussed that patience isn't merely waiting, but what you do while you wait, as you wait with triumphant joy. Maybe the family that is waiting on their new home to be built spends time shopping for furniture and other things they anticipate bringing into the home. Maybe they spend time creating a family mural to commemorate their new beginning. About the woman waiting on her car to be repaired, maybe she takes advantage of this time to connect with a co-worker she believes could use a friend or some support by carpooling with her to get to work. And for the wife waiting for her husband to come around, she spends time continuing to better herself realizing that a better version of herself only further positions them to have a successful, fruitful relationship.

What are some things you can do while you wait concerning those areas you are impatient in?

_____

_____

_____

_____

_____

Declaration

God, I desire to be disciplined in patient endurance. I trust in Your plan and process for me. You pay intimate attention to my desires and seek out a way of allowing me to not only obtain them but to operate with the character to sustain and enjoy them. I call on You to help me to wait in triumphant joy for your promises. Give me the wisdom and insight to know what to work on while I wait. I will not allow impatience to lead me to forfeit the fulfillment of having those things You desire to bless me with. Everything that blesses my relationship and honors You is worth the wait. Everything that You are building within me is for my good and I will receive those things I've waited for at the right time. I relinquish the desire to control, and I will build my trust in You and Your ways. I will develop the spiritual maturity necessary to obtain and keep a healthy relationship. Amen.

Chapter 2:

Love is Kind

Chapter 2
LOVE IS KIND

When we are courting, we feel led to do a lot of nice things for each other. The guy (well, some of us) will open doors for her to enter. She will cook his favorite meal and send him sweet messages. He will occasionally buy her flowers. All the while, as these things are happening, we talk to our family and friends about them. Do you know what we say about them? We say that they are so *nice*. We never say that they are so *kind*. Yet, we mistakenly proceed in our relationships believing that being nice and being kind are one in the same.

Early in our marriage, I did a lot of *stuff*. I would buy things. I would cook things. I would say nice things. I did all these things that were nice towards my wife, but I really wasn't being kind; however, I expected the fruit in the relationship that kindness reaps. So, when I did not see the fruit, being the wise man that I was, I blamed her and resented her for the lack of fruit. How dare she not feel connected and intimate after all the nice things I was doing for her. Unfortunately, I am not the only person who falls victim to this jaded perspective of what kindness really is.

In the book, we uncovered that one necessary ingredient for kindness is that we place value and importance on another person's feelings, circumstances and desires. Had I acknowledged any of these areas for my wife? To be honest, I was aware of some of them, but they were met with critiques and criticisms. Instead of understanding why she would feel certain ways, I spent more time answering for myself *if* she was justified to feel the ways she was feeling. As I write this, I feel less and less like your model husband, but I had to face my reality. At least, I was aware of some of her professed feelings, circumstances and desires. With a changed mindset, I now had accomplished half the battle of being kind to my wife.

Getting the Insight
What are some feelings, circumstances and desires your significant other has voiced in the past?

_____

_____

_____

_____

Chapter 2

Early on in my marriage, the problem wasn't that nice acts are wrong. The problem was that the nice acts I committed had no intentional targets. Acts of kindness are nice, specific acts that address specific needs. If my wife has work to bring home, I can take care of things around the house that she usually would do so that she could focus. I could also make sure the children have things to do so that they are not being a distraction. If she is lacking confidence in a specific area, I can remind her of all the wonderful strengths she possesses in those areas. Men, I strongly urge you to choose this route instead of frowning upon her lack of confidence. The Bible instructs us to encourage each other daily for a good reason.

There was one tragic incident that produced an opportunity to honor my wife. Some years ago, she lost a very close friend and co-worker to a horrific murder. He was a young and caring guy with a heart of gold, especially towards children. He had honestly been a viable encouragement for her, especially in a time where I was not being so encouraging. She was utterly torn apart at the loss. When it happened, I bought her a plant and a card and just listened when she needed to pour her feelings out. I'm thankful that God also put it on my heart to recognize that two dates would return some of these feelings: his birthday and the anniversary of his death. For the anniversary of his death, I had flowers and a card delivered to her job, just to let her know that I would be praying for her and thinking about her as that day would be reflected on. For her birthday (which is close to his birthdate), I got her a locket with a picture of the two of them together as a reminder that he would live on through all her memories of him. I felt honored to see her wear the locket. To me, it meant that the token truly mattered to her. It was a kind and selfless act. Whether in the presence of a tragic moment, the pursuit of a new dream or just a moment of insecurity, I desire to understand my wife and do anything I can to let her know that those moments matter to me.

Make It Count

What can you do to meet or support the feelings, circumstances and desires of your significant other that was voiced earlier?

_____

_____

_____

_____

_____

_____

In our feelings, the world admonishes us to protect ourselves when offended by withholding things from those we have a relationship with. However, the virtue of love admonishes us to lean in greater in these moments. Undeserved kindness is the best opportunity for love to operate in the hearts of those we care about. Kindness is the doorway to repentance. I can speak from experience. One thing that promoted so much change in my heart was the level of kindness my wife exercised in a moment when I knew I deserved so much less. I felt ashamed – not the type of shame that makes you run away but the type of shame that makes you tell yourself that you want to do better. True enough, had she decided to withdraw and simply express her hurt, anger and disgust, I would have felt shame as well, but that type of shame pushes you away. If we desire a healthy, successful relationship, our actions should be geared towards drawing us closer. These choices are evidence of maturity in our hearts and ultimately in the character of our relationships.

Activity
You've Reflected. Now Research

Remember, good acts that do not directly serve a need are at best nice gestures. The greater the clarity of the needs and how to meet them, the better we'll be at offering kindness. Share with your mate what you believe are your opportunities. Give them the opportunity to validate your understanding and/or offer more specifics and insight. Remember, their needs are based on their own values and desires. Work to understand their needs, not to invalidate them. If there is any area you don't fully understand or simply need assistance with, ask for their continued guidance and input in that area.

This is also a good time to share your own needs. This isn't a time to complain and talk about what has or has not happened. Simply, voice your values and desires. Be willing to clarify and offer support on their journey to understanding how to meet your needs.

Chapter 2

Be Kind, Rewind

Go back to a time someone (preferably your significant other) has wronged you or hurt you. How did you respond? Were your actions kind or did you attack or withhold due to the offense? What could you have done to meet a need at that time to communicate your unconditional love towards them? If you were not kind, what did your reaction produce in the relationship? Did it help or hurt your development?

_____
_____
_____
_____
_____
_____
_____
_____
_____
_____
_____
_____

Before you become overwhelmed with a misinterpretation of what kindness is, it should be clarified that being kind isn't about being a genie and granting every request that someone could make. Being kind is about being aware enough to see and meet the depths of your significant other's needs. We need encouragement. We need affirmation. We need help and support in a lot of areas. Being kind understands these needs and sees to it that we partner with the overall desire that the lives of our significant others are fulfilled. If you consider that these are needs and not merely just wants, you maintain the health of your relationship by not tempting your significant other to have these needs met outside of your relationship where you should be the supplier of that help.

Don't Mistake My Kindness for Weakness

Someone read the title of this section and shouted, "Yeah!" We have made this statement so many times, and we might not realize the idea we are ultimately selling when we say this. We make these statements when we want people to know that we will not be taken advantage of and that we can and will act otherwise if we feel it is necessary. Hopefully, with the clarity of understanding that being kind isn't simply doing nice things for people, we can see that there is no being mistreated when we are being kind. With God commanding us to be kind to our enemies, who obviously have no intentional desire to do well towards us, we do not need to be concerned with being mistreated by those we call friends or our lovers. It is not about their intentions; it is about our intentions. To be kind is an act of strength, not weakness. To falter in our kindness is a sign of spiritual weakness.

Remember, all the areas you wrote down (and perhaps even more areas) are areas of need. Even if we were are angry at our children, it would be considered cruel to deny them food, so cruel that Child Protective Services would investigate and possibly relieve us of our children. Consider that you are denying your significant other "food" that we are capable of supplying when we withhold in these areas due to our anger. A starving person may eventually resort to theft to eat a meal. What do you believe the possibilities are when we starve each other of these needs in our relationships? If you want your relationship to work out, acknowledge this area as a non-negotiable and be kind.

Let It Flow

Some of us struggle in offering underserved kindness. Our hearts are hardened, and our hurt is deep. We want the picture of kindness to be equal, so we hold back because we believe they are not focused on being kind to us. However, your significant other should not be the source of your ability nor of your willingness to be kind towards them. God is. God's liberal kindness towards us should be our source to be liberally kind towards others, especially those we profess to love. God has been so kind to us though we, ourselves, are underserving of His kindness. We could never pay Him back, so He asks us to pay it forward to those around us.

If you have never taken the time to acknowledge just how kind and graceful God has been to you, being kind to others will be a great challenge. If you are ungrateful of His kindness, it will also allow your heart to harden when asked to be kind towards others who may be undeserving of your kindness. This is a recipe for disaster in all our relationships if this never gets corrected.

Chapter 2

To hopefully offset this hardened mindset, I want you to write God a sincere letter and acknowledge the specific ways you have seen Him be kind to you and your life, from the salvation He offered your spirit to any personal, specific thing you've witnessed happen in your life.

Dear God,

_____
_____
_____
_____
_____
_____
_____
_____
_____
_____
_____
_____
_____
_____
_____
_____
_____
_____
_____
_____
_____

Declaration

Father, I will consistently mediate on your unending loving kindness towards me. I will allow it to fuel my kindness towards others, especially those I proclaim to matter the most to me. Through meditating on Your word and being present with my significant other, I will become ingenious at identifying and meeting his/her needs. During times when he/she has acted in such a way to hurt or offend me, I will lean in further to continue to meet his/her needs, using it as an opportunity to draw us closer and not further away. God, receive my unconditional acts of kindness towards them as my personal acknowledgment and gratitude towards Your kindness towards me. Discipline me to the point that kindness is the outward reflection of the maturity of my heart. Amen.

Chapter 3:

Love Does Not Envy

Chapter 3
LOVE DOES NOT ENVY

You are sitting at a restaurant of your choice. You are greeted by the waiter, and he takes your order. A short moment later, he brings out your food. As the steam elevates off the plate, you take in the aroma and say your grace. Afterwards, you take your first bite and a surge of flavor enters in, so much that the tables near you can hear your audible appreciation for your food. As you continue to eat, the waiter brings out an order for someone sitting near you. It looks so much more appealing than what you ordered. The plate is sizzling and the look on the other patron's face is that of excitement. Now, you wish you had ordered what they ordered. You continue to eat, but you are not enjoying your food as much as you did with your first bite. Now, it is just a matter of not wasting your money and making sure you are at least not hungry anymore. That, my friend, is the deterioration of life due to envy.

Envy is a feeling of discontent or covetousness with regard to another's advantages, success, possessions, etc. Look back at the restaurant example. You ordered exactly what you wanted. You were even pleased with it when you received your meal. However, the presentation and perceived happiness of the other person seemed to tower over that of your own so much that you could no longer enjoy what you had on the same level of satisfaction that you originally contained. In the book, we talked about two indicators or ways in which we display envy within our relationships.

We envy when we place more value on the thing or experience we presently covet and overlook the value of the things or experiences we currently possess. Was it because the dish originally ordered hadn't lived up to expectations? Absolutely not. The first bite was sensational, but envy has a way of downplaying great things we already possess. We cannot enjoy being healthy because we are not muscle bound. We cannot enjoy being well off financially because we are not filthy rich enough to buy whatever we want like some people can. In our relationships, we cannot enjoy hugs, kisses and shoulder rubs because somebody else is having sex every three days. We cannot enjoy hanging out at the local park because other people are traveling to exotic places to spend time together. Other people seem to laugh more, take more pictures, and openly communicate affection and appreciation and a host of other things that seem to appear to make their relationships more exciting and fulfilling than ours, so we no longer enjoy what we do have on our plates.

Chapter 3

The Apple of Your Eye

Adam and Eve had rights and access to everything in the Garden of Eden except for one tree. They voided access to all they had for the one thing that they didn't have. According to this first indicator, what things do you presently not possess that make it challenging to enjoy what you do have? What things about your relationship are you waiting on to become better before you feel excited about the other elements of your relationship?

_____

_____

_____

_____

_____

_____

_____

_____

_____

_____

We envy when we open the door for resentment towards whatever we perceive is the reason we don't have the things or experiences we wish we had. Have you ever faulted your significant other for the reason you all's lifestyle isn't like others? He can't keep a job. She does not have the degrees to get a job that really pays enough for us to do more. Have you ever faulted your mate because the energy in your relationship is not like you perceive others are? He is such a home body; that is why you never go anywhere. She is such a square; she'd never dance like that with you. He's too uptight. You all can never just have fun.

The reality is that these things may have a level of "reality" about them. She may be too shy to dance. He may not like going places. There is another reality that is not being looked at which is the fact that there must be something amazing about them that led you to decide to be with them. You ordered the food that you wanted, metaphorically speaking. You resent your choice, now, because somebody else's life looks better. You no longer enjoy what you originally decided that you wanted.

In what ways and in what areas have you resented elements of your relationship and/or your significant other because you believe it is the reason you cannot or have not obtained other things that you desire?

_____
_____
_____
_____
_____
_____
_____
_____

Envy – The Dark Gateway

What I have discovered in my own life is that acting in envy produces the darkest of agendas. The Bible even states that where envy is every evil is there (James 3:16). When envy births lust and resentment, they combine to produce a formula for destruction. We begin to selfishly seek after the things we lust. We begin to tear down the things we resent for standing in the way of what we are after. When you are thinking about going out and you know he is not going to want to go, you become disgruntled and unloving in your language. Intimacy and connectivity is far from your desires and aspirations. You have a goal: get away from him because he is the reason you haven't went out and had fun. To find time for "fun" things, the first thing you become willing to sacrifice is time with him.

You resent the fact that she is not making enough money for you all to live a certain way. You decide that you are going to live the way you desire no matter what. Lustfully and with determination, you decide to work more hours and take on more jobs. Of course, the person that now gets less time for you to meet her needs is the woman you professed to love. Your mindset is that she is now minimized to a charity case. "I'm pulling all of the weight. She should understand that, and if she doesn't, it is her issue and not mine."

Notice in both scenarios, we decide to focus on obtaining the thing we envy, and we destroy or take away from something else we once valued (usually the focal point of our resentment). Make no mistake about it, acts of envy materialize into sin, which a

Chapter 3

good friend taught me means in a simple translation we are "missing the mark." However, it is still good to preferable use the word *sin* in efforts to appropriately acknowledge the level of wrong that is introduced so that we can be more compelled in our hearts to turn away from them and "get back on target."

What are ways you have "missed the mark" or sinned out of envy towards something you have desired?

_____
_____
_____
_____
_____
_____
_____
_____
_____
_____
_____

The reason love does not envy is because envy is an evil, hurtful energy. In consideration of God, the people we love and ourselves, we should have a strong desire to cast away any envy within our hearts. It is not to be taken lightly. Remember, Cain's envy turned to jealousy and ultimately led to murder. Even if you never commit physical murder, you will kill and destroy your relationships and your opportunity to be authentically fulfilled in life.

Pray this prayer with me:

Heavenly Father, I see envy for the evil thing that it is. I ask for forgiveness for any time that I have acted out of envy. What I have torn down or destroyed, I need your help to restore those things in my life and in my relationships. In the future, help me to quickly acknowledge envy rising out of me so that I may rebuke it and turn away from it. It is in Jesus' name that I pray. Amen.

The Cure

Where envy is a poison in our hearts and in our relationships, there is a cure: become a *grateful-list*. A grateful-list is someone who has a proclivity to meditate on those things he/she is grateful for in his/her life. It is essentially impossible to be envious and be grateful at the same time. I cannot be envious of another's relationship when my mind is focused on all the blessings of my own relationship. So, how do we cure envy? By being grateful.

Make a Grateful List:
Write out the things that you appreciate about your life, your relationship and your significant other.

_____
_____
_____
_____
_____
_____
_____
_____
_____
_____
_____
_____
_____
_____
_____
_____
_____
_____

Activity
Keep the momentum going. Plan a date, buy a card, write a letter or simply have a conversation with your significant other regarding everything on your list.

Chapter 3

Moving Forward Quick Tip

You may not always have the list you created handy when envy attempts to rise. Life and circumstances may also change. To further offset envy and its schemes, simply learn to genuinely say "thank you" for the things you appreciate, no matter how often they happen. If she cooks a meal for you, thank her. When he takes out the trash, thank him. When she celebrates your accomplishments at work, say "thank you." When he listens to how your day went, say "thank you." Do not become numb to the great things that happen because they happen regularly. I once went through a spell in life where I was close to homeless. I honestly didn't know what I would eat and how much I would eat from day to day. The posture of my heart became different when I said grace over my meals. Some meals were great. Some, honestly, were not so great, but I thanked God, anyway. Because of that experience, I reflect on that time and continue to genuinely thank God for providing food for my plate. For the common things that are good in your relationship, be grateful that they are in fact common. Genuinely thank God and your significant other for those things regularly as much as they happen and witness the posture of your heart change.

Scarcity is a Seed for Envy

The reality is that it is possible to have physical scarcity in our lives and in our relationships. We may be living check to check. We may not have children yet, though we desire to. We may not spend as much time together as we would like due to jobs or other responsibilities. Scarcity is a real thing. Of course, I could say that God still provides everything we need, which is true, but that doesn't always take away the desire for more. So, what I want us to do is look at a few scenarios of scarcity to see how God suggests we deal with it as opposed to giving ourselves over to it and envy others who have more.

2 Kings 4:1-7 The Widow's Oil

Now, in these scriptures, a widow owes a debt for a loan and the debt collectors are aiming at taking her sons to settle the debt. She comes to Elisha, the prophet, and asks for his assistance. He asks her what she has, and she responds saying "nothing in the house but a small jar of olive oil." He advises her to go borrow a lot of jars and then close the door behind her and pour the oil into the jars until all of them are filled. She was able to do just as Elisha had instructed her to do.

So here are the principles we gather from this lesson. First, in her scarcity, she sought help. We do not have to remain silent about a lack of finances, a lack of intimacy in our relationships or even a lack of vision. It is also important to consider that she sought help from a messenger of God. We do not want just anybody's help. We want help from someone who will stand on God's word in their advice and instruction. The world also has suggestions on solving our needs, but that advice can lead to further misfortune and destruction. Secondly, in faith, she acted on what was advised, regardless of how far-fetched it may have seemed. We desire intimacy, and someone says, "pray together." We may think, "How is that going to do anything for our intimacy problems." If it doesn't step outside of God's commands for us, why not have faith that it is possible for it to work. Whether God tells you to gather jars, take some time away from work, tithe, cook a meal for them every day this week, or simply share kind words, in faith, God will increase us in those areas all the while increasing our faith in Him at the same time.

Matthew 14:13 – 21 – Five Thousand Fed

Of course, this is one of the most famous stories in the Bible. Thousands are gathered before Jesus as he heals their sick. The hour is growing late, and the disciples suggest the crowd is released to go into the city to buy something to eat. Jesus instructs them to feed the crowd instead and the disciples search and suggest that two fish and five loaves of bread are not enough to feed five thousand men and their women and children. Jesus asks them to bring the food to Him. He thanks God for it, blesses and breaks it. He hands it to the disciples to distribute and they feed everyone and gather twelve baskets of leftovers.

When we witness scarcity in our lives, a huge thing to consider is that the scarcity is scarce outside of God's hands. It is our limited, logical brains that are ultimately scarce in uncovering the spans and capacity of God's unlimited power and resources. You and your mate only have a little time together? Give that time together to God? You are living check to check? Give your money over to how God instructs us to steward our money. Your intimacy is low? Give your connection over to God. Thank Him for you all's relationship and bless it.

The other thing to note is that Jesus turns and places what He has blessed back in the hands of those who questioned the sustainability of what they possessed to begin with, and they distributed the food. Once God says it is enough, will you go back into your relationships with an "it is enough" attitude, realizing that with God's supernatural hand on it, it is more than enough. You will be amazed at the impact of ten minutes of intentional time with your spouse can make over the grand scheme of you all's relationship. One resume sent to the right companies can significantly change your financial situation. One heartfelt conversation can magnify the intimacy in your relationship.

Chapter 3

So above all, when we view scarcity, instead of envying others who seemingly have more or better things, understand that, in faith, in God's hands, we always have more than enough. Essentially, we thank God for what we do have, ask Him to bless it, and then witness Him magnify the presence of those things as we go back into our relationships with a renewed mindset.

Declaration

Lord, I ask you to open my heart to see the value in the things and people you have already positioned in my life. In gratitude, I will maximize the opportunities that are already before me. I will celebrate what others are positioned to do in their lives without coveting those things. I have faith and trust that greater blessings for me will be released in their appropriate seasons. You are the key holder to all that is good for me, so I will turn to you for my requests and I will follow your plans. Ultimately, the joy of my life is your presence in my life. Everything else of value, I acknowledge as your favor in my life. Help me to remember your favor, daily. Help me to honor you by having a spirit of thanksgiving when I view my significant other, our children, our current financial status, and our lifestyle. Improving in these areas requires Your wisdom and my faith that they will truly increase. Let me not turn away from You and the things You value to pursue what I, in my limited understanding, perceive as better. I cast away any envy that has driven me away from You and my significant other, and I pray that my gratitude towards both of you will draw us all back together.

Chapter 4:

It Does Not Boast

Chapter 4
IT DOES NOT BOAST

Boast - to speak with exaggeration and excessive pride, especially about oneself.

It feels good to feel good about oneself. Doesn't it? In sports and in any other competitive fields, it feels good to proclaim to be the greatest. When we earn that bonus, we feel good knowing that our hard work paid off and that our contributions are appreciated. As children, we find gratitude in knowing that our parents are proud of us. This desire alone is really not a problem. The problem enters when we begin to boast about who we are and our accomplishments. As indicated by the definition, boasting occurs when we exaggerate what we've done or when we have excessive pride in what we've done.

When I first married my wife, I had a deep desire to be a good husband for her. I appreciated that she appreciated me. I wanted to do and say things that would make her happy. There are many moments when she would be impressed with something I did: repairing something around the house, cooking a nice meal, or simply paying her a heartfelt compliment. However, my boasting took place during times she expressed a lack in an area. My boasting took place when I felt like she was refusing to meet a need or desire of mine. Perhaps, when she expressed disappointment, I associated that disappointment with my identity. I did not want to feel like less than a man. I did not want to feel like less than a good husband. In fear of being a failure, instead of rising to the need, I scrutinized her for focusing on that need. "She doesn't appreciate all that I do for her." This was the thought in my mind. This may not directly appear to be boasting, but "all that I do for her" may subjectively amount to more in my head than it did in hers. I mean, is not thinking that she had no right to desire more an exaggeration of what I was providing as a husband at the time? Could I have really mastered marriage in such a short span of time? Had I not become excessively prideful in what I had accomplished in our marriage? As for my request from her, was I truly entitled to demand those desires be met based off my own deeds and worth? Boasting entered our marriage at a very early period.

No Robots, No Slaves

Are there areas in your relationship you have placed demands and have overlooked your significant other's regular choice to value you and take care of you in that area? Write down any area of your relationship where you have instituted this demand at the detriment of valuing what your significant other is already contributing.

_____
_____
_____
_____
_____
_____
_____
_____
_____
_____

The Rebel

Have you considered that you are already doing enough so much that you are not desiring or making it a priority to progress in your relationship? Are you forcing your mate to settle for less when you can or should do more because you rather them be without than strive to be better? Write down anything you have intentionally withheld from your significant other, forcing them to settle for what you are contributing.

_____
_____
_____
_____
_____
_____
_____
_____

Chapter 4

Humility's Door

Humility is the antidote to operating in excessive pride. In moments where we want to boast in who we are and either demand something from them or refuse something they have requested, it is a good opportunity to consider our imperfections, our mistakes, and our humanity. I may feel entitled to limit the extracurricular activities in our marriage, but if I acknowledge just how much time I put into things outside of our marriage, I can accept how it could appear that I have prioritized other things above her. I could demand sex as a natural need of a man, but I can also acknowledge that I'm still learning how to meet her intimate needs outside of sex, which are more important to most women. On either side, in humility, we would discover that we have a reason to be less demanding of things we want and need and be more intentional on meeting their needs and wants. Again, where boasting blinds us from this fact, humility opens the door for a healthier perspective.

Define your faults and shortcomings. Humbly express gratitude that your significant other has offered you grace, compassion, support and/or forgiveness in those areas.

_____
_____
_____
_____
_____
_____
_____
_____
_____

The Law and Lesson of Works

For it is by grace you have been saved, through faith and this is not from yourselves, it is the gift of God - not by works, so that no one can boast. ~ Ephesians 2:8-9

In many marriages, works have been misappropriated. The misappropriation is not necessarily in the lack of works but in where the value of the works has been attributed. In unhealthy relationships, the person committing the works places more value in themselves for having done the work. In healthy relationships, the person committing the works does so as an expression of value of the one for whom he does the works. When I first married my wife, remember, I wanted to be a good husband. While I was committing good works, I used them to identify myself as a good husband. As I continued with this mindset, I drifted further and further away from committing good works as an expression of her being the love of my life.

Works alone may be considered amoral. The *why* behind our acts will ultimately produce its fruit in our relationships. Our works committed in pure love is the healthiest approach to our relationships. The idea that our works could ever put us in position to demand anything from our mates in our relationships creates a business contract and not that of an intimate relationship. No matter how many works we commit, we commit them in gratitude to God for placing someone in our lives that causes us to humble ourselves, acknowledge their worth to us, and serve them.

Write out the things you do (works) in your relationship and follow them with a strong "because" statement. Realize that the acts are subjugated to the reasons and desires and not vise-versa.

Example: When my wife expresses a desire for something tangible, I try to provide it BECAUSE every one of her desires matter to me and where as she may think she has to do without those things, I want her to know that I desire to make those things happen for her, hoping those things will add a smile to her face and communicate that her desires are important to me.

_____

_____

_____

_____

_____

_____

_____

_____

Granting the Increase

As the inner child never fully dies, we can get disappointed when it seems that our works aren't being appreciated and celebrated on the level that we believe they should. We become dismayed when our acts aren't producing the intimacy we desire. If you haven't already discovered each other's love languages as author Gary Chapman highlights in his book *The Five Love Languages*, it is a very practical book to read and follow. For some of us who are aware of the love languages, even when we try to speak in their love language, it seems we are still unsuccessful in producing results. She loves words of affirmation, but she has a hard time believing me when I tell her that she's beautiful and that she is talented. He is a quality time type of man, but even as you set time aside for the two of you, you still feel distant during that time together.

I planted the seed, Apollos watered it, but God has been making it grow. So neither the one who plants nor the one who waters is anything, but only God, who makes them grow.
~ I Corinthians 3:6-7

Our works are seeds planted in our relationships. Seeds of bad works will eventually reap bad fruit. Seeds of good works will eventually reap good fruit. To prevent the temptation to boast, God has taken dominion over the growth plan of our relationships. Whereas we are enabled to plant seeds, God supervises the supernatural ingredients to grow our relationships and our intimacy. Consider God the mediator and regulator. Our relationships are not designed to be healthy without His presence. Commit your works as acts of faith that God is honoring your efforts and securing the eventual growth of the relationship. Just remember, your works will never be greater than the one you do it for and unto God who grants the increase.

Pray this prayer:
Heavenly Father, bring to my memory the humble reasons for which I commit my works. Strengthen me to trust that You are granting the increase in our relationship. In Your love and grace, keep me humble that I may continue to serve the love of my life and honor You with my life. Amen.

Declaration

From this day moving forward, I will no longer place my value on my works. My identity and value are found in who God says I am and in nothing else. Therefore, I can freely and liberally commit my works to those I love and whom God designates. I will be intentional in producing works in my relationship, not to be glorified, but to serve the one I love. My spouse is worth it to me. I will exercise patience as my significant other continues to grow and mature with me. Whereas I will continue to express desires and continue to press closer in intimacy, I will not make tyrant demands. I will also humbly hear my significant other as they help me to further understand their needs and desires.

Chapter 5:

Love is not Proud

Chapter 5
LOVE IS NOT PROUD

The journey through the book and this workbook is geared towards gaining a deeper understanding of what love is to produce healthier relationships. We would like to believe that our ability to love our significant other rests on how much we work together, but the reality is that our ability to love solely rests upon our spiritual maturity. Working well together is the byproduct of spiritual maturity. The more we trust and adhere to how the Word of God commands our lives the more we are enabled to love each other, among many other things God has called us to do as His children.

It was particularly important to bring up this fact in this chapter because there is a trait in our flesh that stubbornly, viciously fights against this spiritual maturity: pride.

Pride - having, proceeding from or showing a high opinion of one's own dignity, importance or superiority.

Have you ever found yourself concerned about who was "winning" in the relationship? Who won the argument? Who gets their way more than the other person? Have you ever asked yourself why you are even keeping score? Have you ever heard the instructions from a preacher or someone else with a sound mind and refused to follow those instructions to the detriment of your relationship? Have you ever heard a voice in your mind suggesting you do something nice for your significant other or to apologize for your role in a given situation and you decided to ignore that voice?

I knew my wife wanted help with keeping the kitchen clean. I considered myself too tired to focus on that. It could get done when it got done. I told myself that if I did it, then she would just ask me to do something else. I told myself that I work just like she works, and I was entitled to a break. I'm pretty sure I am not winning the husband of the year award as you read this. I knew my voice had elevated during our last conversation. I saw her spirit drop. There was a voice inside that said that I should apologize, but I was still upset. "She upset me, and a raised voice is something she should anticipate when she upsets me. She hurt my feelings, too, and I don't see her apologizing to me." Yep, by this time, I don't believe I was even fit for a nomination for the award. It is one thing to be unaware of the right thing to do, but there are times we know exactly what the right thing to do is and we refuse to do it.

Chapter 5

What area are you fighting the right thing to do even though you are aware that that is what you should be doing? What is your honest reason? What do you believe God has to say about it and what does that mean to you? Have an open and honest conversation with God in this area. Pray to hear from Him.

_____
_____
_____
_____
_____
_____
_____
_____
_____
_____
_____

The Punisher

Everyone proud in heart is an abomination to the Lord; though they join forces, none will go unpunished. ~ Proverbs 16:5

I believe that most of the bad we witness and even experience in life is the consequence of sin. Often, we look at all the wrong in the world and say that God is punishing us for our actions, but the reality is that we are witnessing the effects of our actions. Murder is the effect of anger and rage. Fatherless children are the effect of lustful relationships (not in all cases). War is the effect of greed and selfish ambition (not in all cases, again). We feel the pain, but it is not God inflicting the pain. It is our sin. However, there is a group of people that God specifically punishes: the proud.

Punishment - a penalty inflicted for an offense.

The proud in heart are an offense to God. When we operate in pride in our lives, we should know that God is coming for us. Why? The reason is pride causes us to be our own "god" in certain areas of our lives. The true living God has a history of tearing down any idol god that has been placed above Him.

You know, we may think that Satan is foolish for fighting a battle he has already lost. How could he ever speculate that he could defeat God? It is not about the possibility of being able to defeat God. Satan has pride. How foolish is it of us to knowingly consider ourselves to be superior rather than to humbly do the things that God asked us to do for one another? Are we wiser than God? Stronger than God? Can we outrun God? Can we defeat God? Can our plans succeed without Him? The answer to all these questions is no; however, our pride causes us to choose our own way over God's way.

Let's have a moment of honesty.

Are there any methods, contrary to God's methods, that you utilize in your relationship believing they are superior to God's instructions? If so, why? God says a quiet voice turns away an angry wrath (Proverbs 15:1). However, we believe we must dominate their wrath with greater wrath. God's word instructs married people to not separate (I Corinthians 7:10), but in difficult moments we separate anyway. There are many other examples. Honestly, is there any method outside of God's will for you in your relationship that you trust in more? Talk about it.

_____

_____

_____

_____

_____

_____

_____

_____

_____

_____

_____

Chapter 5

The Schemes of Pride

We can say that pride is a double negative. God elects to punish the proud, and, just as it is with every sin, there are effects and consequences birthed out of acts of pride. God will not attack your marriage or punish your relationship because of your pride. Your pride does that job all by itself. God desires to destroy the pride, not you. God desires to walk in covenant with you and your marriage, not to tear it apart. We must face that there are some adverse effects to our well-being when pride dictates our actions.

In my own pride, I have verbally torn down the well-being of my wife to protect my vulnerable weaknesses. In my own pride, I have cheated us out of enjoying great milestones together by assuming all the credit. In my own pride, I have communicated, at times, more disdain for our relationship, which drove my wife away from me. In my own pride, I have refused to work on healing. I have denied help from others. I have lashed out at everyone else for their faults. I've embraced those who falsely supported my "superior" mindset. All these things hurt my relationship, my wife, and ultimately me. In the moment, pride seems to offer me strength, confidence, and even protection. As time plays out, it ultimately reveals my weakness and insecurity. Pride may have built a wall, but the wall doesn't protect but rather it imprisons.

What did your pride do?

What have you done in your pride? What have been the effects of your actions in your relationship? Write them down and go to your mate, humble yourself, and apologize for committing acts that could have destroyed them and your relationship.

_____
_____
_____
_____
_____
_____
_____
_____

Pray It Away

Humbling yourself before God is a great start to walking away from the pride in your life. Say this prayer out loud:

Heavenly father, I bow my head in reverence to Your infinite wisdom and power. Your ways are not my ways. They are far greater. I apologize for the times I trusted more in my feelings, my emotions, and in my limited knowledge. I apologize for trusting in my own methods of protection than in being covered by You. I apologize for trusting in my own methods for success than in doing what You commanded me to do. I apologize for any act of pride I've done to challenge my relationship with You and my spouse. I need You now more than ever to help me repair the destruction. Strengthen the Holy Spirit in me to lean not unto my own understanding but in all my ways acknowledge You. Thank you for Your grace and mercy. You could have taken me out. You could have allowed me to completely fall. However, you loved me enough to cover me in my folly. Though I don't deserve You, I am grateful I have You as my Heavenly Father. I appreciate the blessings You surround me in, especially in my relationship. God, I seek Your glory and not Your punishment. I willingly accept Your discipline and correction because I genuinely desire to be better. Because You believe in me, I am willing to make the effort. In moments where my pride rises, please give me the strength to subdue it. I want Your spirit to reign in me. In Jesus name I pray, Amen.

Declaration

My pride will not dictate how I operate in my relationship. I am not afraid to expose my vulnerable and weak areas to my significant other. I am not superior. I'm human. I am not afraid of revealing my need for God's wisdom, mercy, grace and love. I need Him to drive my compassion and humility in my relationship. I will develop the posture of gratitude and appreciation towards God and my significant other. We are on a journey together. I will use my strengths to support and not to dominate in my relationship. My aim is not to be celebrated separately, but that we celebrate collectively all that God is doing in our lives. God reigns over me. As I submit to Him, He will fulfill all the promises of His Word.

Chapter 6:

Love is not Rude

LOVE IS NOT RUDE

Call it my skepticism or paranoia, but I have this suspicion that some of us will read this material and negate its importance. I believe some of us will target what appears to be the main issues in our relationship. I can see someone saying, "We're not struggling in our relationship because I can be rude at times. They can get over that. We have bigger problems that need to be addressed." Two things: first, it is the small termites that tear down the whole building. Being rude may seem insignificant, but I wouldn't overlook the Word of God's intention to state that love is not rude. Secondly, if there are more major things to do in our relationships, how can we be trusted to commit to them when we do not address the things we already know to do? Surely, our heartfelt admiration and affection towards our significant others are not instructing us to be rude. In fact, they are surely instructing us to be otherwise. If we would not listen to those instructions, we will not adhere to what one may consider to be greater instructions.

A great discipline is required to acknowledge and adhere to these principles. As I stated in the book, people in healthy relationships did not luckily find the right one; they decided to do it the right way with the one they were with. You can elect to not focus on one area or another, but those who are committed to making their relationships and marriages healthier will address anything that stands between them and a flourishing relationship, including the seemingly small things. We can have all the desire in the world to have a great relationship, but without the conviction to do something about it, things will not get better.

So, What Are You Saying?

There was a time I was having a conversation with my wife. It wasn't the easiest of conversations to have. She was at work, but I called her anyway so that negative thoughts would not fester and inhibit my ability to communicate with her later concerning the topic. She listened attentively and though she did not defend herself against what was being expressed, her tone became short, irritable and distant. Her word choice was not disrespectful or demeaning, but her tone communicated much more than what the words, themselves, communicated. Because of her tone, I believed my concerns and intentions were not received well. Her tone added to my frustration and fatigue regarding the situation. It honestly did not motivate me to be vulnerable to her again. Being rude is more than what we say but also how we say it. I can recall times my wife asked me a question and I gave her the right answer, but my tone also said, "I

Chapter 6

can't believe you didn't know that. Who are you?" Our tones are what suggest we are being sarcastic or demeaning, which are both strong traits of being rude.

Take a moment to reflect on times your significant other's tone came off rude more so than what they said. Take a moment to reflect on situations where an inner voice made you respond to simple statements in a rude or demeaning way. If you cannot recall a time your tone has been harmful, ask your mate to bring an occasion to your memory.

_____
_____
_____
_____
_____
_____
_____
_____
_____

Being Blunt vs. Being Direct

I'm also confident that a sizable amount of us do not feel like we should have to walk on eggshells just to address our significant others. We want to feel like we can be open and honest about our concerns. We do not feel it is necessary to treat our significant others like babies when we address them. I do not disagree with this sentiment. At no point in time do we need to address them as babies, but we should address them as valuable and meaningful to our lives. There's a big difference in being blunt and in being direct. Whereas I usually cite the definitions here, for simplicity, I'm going to display the synonyms.

Blunt - Synonyms: dull, insensitive, and pointless

Direct - Synonyms: absolute, sincere, and point-blank

Looking at the synonyms, it appears that they are in fact opposites of each other. When we are being blunt, we make statements like, "You are lazy." If we were being direct, the statement would be, "I really need you to do more around the house." Both are addressing the same issue. While being blunt, we may have been straightforward with our feelings and the conclusion we've come to because of them, but it is insensitive in that there is name-calling. It is dull or pointless because it doesn't deal with the root issue. Further conversation would be needed to even fully understand the true concern. While being direct, we go straight to our concern without creating any energy beyond that of addressing the desire for them doing more around the house. That is the difference between being blunt and being direct.

Recall anything you may have been blunt about and rewrite it to directly address what you really were attempting to convey. Again, if you cannot recall a time, ask your mate if there has been any. Prior to being blunt in the future, remember to use this strategy to gather your thoughts so that you can directly state the true, sincere concern.

What did you say (that was blunt)?

_____
_____
_____
_____

How could you have stated it to be more direct?

_____
_____
_____
_____

As you move forward in your relationship, remember that being blunt is less likely to produce the results you genuinely desire.

Sticks and Stones...

Whoever said that words do not hurt was not receiving hurtful words from someone they care about. If you think your significant other does not care about how you address them, you are gravely mistaken. The reality is that you want those words to matter to them. When I encourage my wife and tell her about all the great things I see in

Chapter 6

her, I want her to know how much I really meant it. I want it to be a source of encouragement for her. How can I have that expectation, hope or desire and not expect rude and harmful words to have an adverse effect on her? We do not get to pick and choose which part of our words will have greater impact. Just as much as we want the words "I love you" to resonate with them, believe that the words, "I hate you" will have an impact as well.

    The reality is that our negative and demeaning words seem to have greater influence and impact than our positive words. There are studies that give evidence that it takes so many more positive words to negate the effect of one negative word. Because we have no discipline over our tongues, we want to demand that they quickly get over our words as quickly as we allowed them to come out of our mouths. No, we're not perfect, and we will at times say things we may wish we could take back. We need forgiveness in our relationships, but it is something that we cannot demand but only give. The other part of asking for forgiveness is to sincerely desire to refrain from committing the act again. It negates an apology if we are going to be perfectly fine with being rude in the future. This realization connects the opening idea that we must address the severity of seemingly simple acts.

Activity

Have you and your mate each take out a sheet of paper. On this paper, write out anything that has ever been said by them that has hurt you. If possible, purchase either sad face stickers or simply some circular dots. For each hurtful item, place those stickers or dots on your face. For each hurtful thing, two things will happen. After you have stated the hurtful thing that was said, you will give them an opportunity to sincerely ask for forgiveness and commit to refraining from hurting you in that way again. After they have done so, you will open your heart to forgiveness by removing the sticker from your face committing to never hold those words against him/her again. You will also give your mate the opportunity to state where you have hurt them in the past so that you can ask for forgiveness and they can also commit to never hold those things against you again.

I'm Sure You're Not Sarcastic at All

As my friends and I were going over the book, one of them suggested that I spell out what sarcasm really is. I did state the definition in the book: "a sharply ironical taunt." I'm sure everybody in the world understands what that means. Just like my personal example in the book, this statement was intentionally made to convey what sarcasm looks like. Do I really believe that everybody in the world understands that definition? If I don't believe it, why wouldn't I simply state that I didn't? What is the actual benefit, if any, of being sarcastic?

Let's breakdown the words used to define sarcasm. *Sharply* in this definition means merciless, caustic, or harsh. *Ironical* means pertaining to, of the nature of, exhibiting, or characterized by mockery. Finally, *taunt* is to find fault in an insulting way. Anybody who did not understand the original definition probably felt insulted that I said everybody should understand it. I drew a harsh conclusion. I didn't mean what I said, hence, the ironical. The statement would cause one to believe that I would find fault in them not knowing. Any comment that you make that fits this criterion is a sarcastic comment. By looking at the traits of a sarcastic comment, hopefully, you can see why it is considered rude and why love would never communicate this way.

Activity

Most people are sarcastic because it simply entertains them. They do not actually mean to be offensive, though it is usually the result, so have some fun with changing your behavior. Like a *swear jar*, establish a *sarcasm jar*. If either of you are sarcastic to each other or anybody else, for that matter, agree on a dollar amount to put inside of the jar. If you happen to speak sarcastically, be sure to correct your language as well. Agree on how the money will be spent: donated to a charity or church, spent on a date night, or whatever else you can agree on. If you do not want to involve money, create special favors (nothing demeaning) that you will owe each other if you speak to each other in a sarcastic way. It could be something as simple as a kiss or cooking a special meal.

Honey, I Shrunk Your Value in My Mind

Being rude is belittling. When we are rude to people, we shrink their significance or importance in our minds. If I am consistently being rude to my wife, without having the audacity to verbally say it, I have reduced her value to me. With her value reduced, she becomes an annoyance, not because of anything she has done, but because my

Chapter 6

thought-life has deteriorated her value in my mind. The ultimate danger in this is that I begin to withhold my best from her. I don't go the extra mile. Service to her becomes a chore, instead of an honor. Without recognizing it, my irritable, rude nature overshadows any "love" I believe I am still showing her. We withdraw. We detach. At the end of the day, being rude is undermining. It is a form of verbal abuse. It is a surefire way to completely damage our relationships.

Proverbs 18:21 instructs that *"death and life are in the power of the tongue, and those who love it and indulge it will eat its fruit and bear the consequences of their words."* Can we expect to use rude words and not bear the fruit of them? What have we put to death in our relationships with rude words? Intimacy? Trust? Safety and security? Just because the first blow doesn't take us out does not mean it is not killing us. I can't continue to stand as a loving husband if I continue to be rude. She cannot stand as a loving wife if she continues to be rude. In rudeness, the presence of love dies.

Why not put this scriptural principle to great use? Yes, there is the awareness of doom and gloom in this scripture, but there is a key word to take ownership of: *power*. We have the power to put something to death or bring something to life embedded in our tongues. Amazing! A bulldozer is built to destroy and demolish. However, it is not a bad invention. After something has been demolished and removed, something new can be built up. If you are like me, there are buildings of hurt, judgement and criticism that have been erected in my relationship. The power of my tongue can destroy and demolish those things. "Baby, I told you that you were not worth it anymore, but that was a lie!" Then, I can build something. "You are the apple of my eye and the woman of my youth. You sustain my desire for passion and love." Keep in mind, rude words didn't kill overnight and neither will life-giving words resurrect as quickly, but just like rude words are promised to kill, life-giving words will give life eventually.

> **Activity**
> Demolition and Construction
>
> This will be more of a lifestyle change than that of a one-time activity. I want you to speak (out loud) against every monument of hurt you may have caused or that you might have felt. Any word you have ever spoken negatively against your spouse, in secret or to his/her face, I want you to go to them and speak the very opposite. If there are certain things that you have said about yourself that position you to be unfit for your relationship, I want you to continuously speak against that identity. Those things that you are desiring for the wellness of your relationship, I want you to speak those things into existence. For as long as it takes to see the fruition and change, I want you to intentionally put to death the undesirable and speak to life the healthiness and success of your relationship. You may not be able to recall every damaging thing you made have said towards your spouse. Ask them to bring to your memory anything you have negatively spoken that continues to live inside of them and haunt their idea of how you see them and how they may view themselves.

There are so many external things that motivate our rude behaviors. Some of us grew up in a rude environment. We witness celebrities and other "successful" people build a following based on their rudeness or despite it. We have seen rudeness displayed in such ways that makes it entertaining or exciting, and we adopt them into our own lives. No matter how common rudeness is for you, be wise and remove it from your character, especially inside of your relationship. Its fruit is death. It does not show honor to the people we are addressing, and it speaks poorly to our own character and identity. We cannot rightly present ourselves as God's representatives and be rude with the same tongue. Love would not do such a thing.

Pray with me:

Lord, I ask for forgiveness for every time I was rude to my spouse and others. Correct my heart. Let my words and the way I use my words honor You and indicate the value that You have placed on Your people. Help me to mend the wounds created by my rude words. Redeem the time lost and close the gap on the distance that has been created. Help my spouse through the healing process. As You create in me a cleaner heart, let it be visible. Replace my language. Help me find healthier ways to communicate my needs, desires, hurts and concerns. Give me new ways to establish humor rather than ridicule my significant other. Help me to be compassionate in areas of their development instead

Chapter 6

of being harsh and critical. Help me to communicate through love and no other form. It is in Jesus' name I pray. Amen.

Declaration

The power of life and death is in my tongue. I will speak life to my relationship. I will speak life into my spouse. I will speak death to all the thoughts and words that have damaged and destroyed my relationship. I will honor and value my spouse in deed and word. I will not overlook the devastating effects of rude words. I will be quick to ask for forgiveness and correct my words if they ever fall short of the value God has placed on anybody. How my words are used defines me and nobody else. My words will reveal that I am a new creature, born and led by Christ, to model His love and compassion towards God's children, especially my spouse.

Chapter 7:

Love is not Self-Seeking

Chapter 7
LOVE IS NOT SELF-SEEKING

If there is any sneaky, little demon in our relationships, lust is it. Lust has a creative way of appearing as love. It has a deceptive way of masking its genuine motives so that the actions appear purely motivated. Not only can we deceive others in our actions, we can deceive ourselves. We will believe we are operating out of love because the "feelings" of love are present during our actions. However, we can find ourselves disappointed when we don't get the reaction or reward we were anticipating from our "acts of love." However, God is never deceived by our actions. Galatians 6:7-9 informs us that God will not be mocked. The seeds we plant are determined by the true motivations of our hearts. We will only reap from our motivations. Selfish or fleshly motives reap destruction. Seeds sown from the spirit reap a harvest.

Moment of Honesty

What has been the motivation behind the things you do in your relationship? What was the response you desired? Have you reaped the fruit you intended to reap? If not, what do you believe is the reason the fruit has not manifested?

_____

_____

_____

_____

_____

_____

_____

The sowing of seeds analogy is profound. You have heard the saying, "You do not plant an apple seed and anticipate an orange tree." However, this seed analogy is not discussing the difference between reaping apples and oranges. It is talking about the difference between reaping good apples and bad apples. Doing the right thing for the wrong reasons produces bad fruit. You may recall from the book that lust aims to please self and love aims to please someone else. Jeremiah 29:11-14 speaks of God's plans and desires to do well unto to us. As you read through the scriptures, His expectation is that we will then "call on [Him]" and afterwards He desires to do even more for us! Usually, our expectations are that we will have the good deeds returned to us. God desires a deeper relationship with us, to walk with us so that He can do even more great things in our lives. Lust drives us in saying, "What's in it for me?" Love drives us in saying, "How can we benefit them?"

What Do You Want

What are you genuinely desiring from your relationship? Be honest. What are your plans?

_____
_____
_____
_____
_____
_____
_____
_____
_____
_____
_____
_____
_____
_____
_____
_____
_____

Chapter 7

> **Activity**
> ## Make Some Plans
>
> God's love for us leads Him to make plans for our lives – great plans. If you follow His model in Jeremiah, He speaks of what He will do for us and how He anticipates we will respond. Once we respond, He even has further plans to do good for our lives. He is consistent about His plans benefiting us. I want you to make plans that benefit your spouse. Once you've made them, I want you to share it with them. I'll give you an example: "I am working on my listening skills and being less critical. I want you to be more willing to talk to me about what is on your mind – good or bad. When you decide to share more with me, I want to understand both your heart and your mind and be aware of how I can personally help you achieve any specific desire or overcome any specific obstacle." Notice the pattern, your actions should lead them to respond. Their response should be an open door for you to do even more for them. You can use this example in your own relationship, but I encourage you to take a moment now and make your own plans for the person you love.
>
> _____
> _____
> _____
> _____
> _____
> _____
> _____
> _____
> _____
> _____

How Do We Know What's Our Priority?

Remember, selfish ambition is a sneaky, little thing. At the beginning of my marriage, I believed all my ambitions were centered around her benefit, but time proved otherwise. In the book, we talked about how delayed fruit is a way of testing our motives. Are our good acts intended to benefit them or to give them a reason to do what we want them to do? A key indicator is whether we withhold the good we desire to do for them as ransom until they do what we want them to do for us. It is impossible to not desire anything from our significant others, but we can either prioritize our needs before theirs or their needs before ours. This is the ultimate test of our motives. When our needs are not being met, we can grow weary. Galatians tells us to not grow weary but believe that the harvest is inevitable and will come in due season – an appropriated time.

Activity
Give it Back

Have you withdrawn an act of love from your spouse or something that makes their lives better? Give it back. Although, this is not in absence of continuing to communicate your needs and desires, to be spiritually mature, we must commit to continuing to do what is healthy for their lives and our relationships. Itemize those things you have taken away (through weariness or spite) and commit to returning it to your relationship. Ask for forgiveness and let your actions demonstrate your change of heart.

_____
_____
_____
_____
_____
_____

Die to What???

So, if you have been a part of any Christian community for any given period, you have probably heard someone say that we need to die to self. What does that mean? Die to self? It is obvious that they are not talking about a physical death. However, if we attempt to ignore our feelings, emotions, hopes, fears and desires, we will find ourselves living in contempt with God and the people around us. Dying to self does not mean ignoring our humanity. To die to self, we must have a death or move away from selfish desire, selfish motivations and self-understanding.

Chapter 7

Selfish desire:

When we crave and long for things that only benefit us, that is selfish desire. To put selfish desire to death, we must let go of craving things that only benefit us and delight in things that benefit others. For selfish desires, we will expense others. For selfless desires, we'll expense ourselves.

What are some things you desire for your spouse? What are some things you know they desire? What are you willing to expend of yourself to help those desires be met?

_____
_____
_____
_____
_____
_____
_____
_____
_____

Selfish motivation:

Selfish motivation is to have our actions driven by our own interest. We only do things when we want something. We only do things when we feel like doing it. We are only motivated to do things if we believe we will gain something of value in return. To put selfish motivation to death, we must find a "why" outside of ourselves, to drive our actions. I recommend pleasing and honoring God as a motivator. In our relationships, there should also be a secondary motivator to drive our actions, something we'll commit to achieving even when we do not feel like doing it. Maybe the "why" is establishing a relational legacy for your children that you did not grow up seeing. Maybe the "why" is offering your spouse the safe place they never had growing up or in any other relationship. We must find a meaningful "why."

What are the "why's" outside of yourself that has motivated you or will now motivate your actions in your relationship?

_____
_____
_____
_____
_____
_____
_____

Self-understanding:

Self-understanding is seeing the world and ourselves solely or predominantly from our own point of view. We limit what is considered normal and right to our own beliefs and opinions. God instructs us to not be dependent on our own understanding but to acknowledge what He says instead, informing us that His ways and thoughts are not like ours. (Proverbs 3:5-6) We must die to our own understanding or otherwise we will rebel against any of His instructions and wisdom that disagrees with what we believe in ourselves. Many of our quarrels in our relationships exist because we have unhealthy or ungodly views on what our relationships should be. I don't necessarily mean ungodly as in being evil. I mean ungodly as in not being merited by His wisdom and intentions concerning relationships. We die to self-understanding so that we may operate with sound judgement and instructions in our lives and concerning those things that matter to us.

What is not working in your relationship? Communication? Financial management? Where have your own personal views proven inadequate to move the relationship forward? Write those areas down here and pray that God strips you of your own understanding and offers His wisdom in those areas.

_____
_____
_____

Chapter 7

_____
_____
_____
_____

Check Please

After a meal has been eaten at a restaurant, perhaps at the end of a date, you usually ask the waiter for the check to prepare to pay for the meal. You may split the check and pay for your own portions, or one person may decide to cover the entire bill. I want you to take this picture and consider what love looks like. Now, for the first meal, it may not matter to you how the check is paid. Either of you could pay or you could split it and you would be perfectly fine. It is those dinners and dates that follow that start to get our attention. "Am I always expected to pay?" "Are we really together if we keep splitting the checks?" We start to look for a pattern or establish a rule to be followed moving forward. Here is what is different about love. Love is not concerned with whose turn it is to "pay" for the situations that arise in our relationships. Love is not being combative about who is loving more than the other person. Love is always charging us to mature in our understanding of what it means and to learn to effectively love the person we say is worth it. The person that has the money in the account is not worried about covering the bill. I promise you, if you are mindful of how much God has done for you, undeservingly, you will have spiritual money in your account to pay the bill for the expenses your mate incurs. God didn't pay the bill and rub it in our faces. Instead, He paid it and made a commitment to move forward in His relationship with us.

What expenses have you paid on behalf of your mate? What expenses haven't you paid that you are in position to pay due to the limitless account of grace that God has given you? Acknowledge those areas here and make a commitment to pay the expense so that you and your spouse can move forward in your relationship. For example, I might say that my wife usually takes the frustration and stress of life out on me. I can pay the expense by understanding the true root and help her navigate through her stress, even when I am not the cause of it.

_____
_____
_____

_____

_____

_____

_____

If we are going to have a healthy relationship, we must learn to serve our significant others selflessly. It can be difficult to continue to do so when some of our deep needs and desires are not being met but remember that love is always driven by what it desires to give and not by what we can receive in return. Even though lust seeks pleasure, it never gets satisfied. Love is satisfying. We must mature and never withhold what love desires to do for others, especially our spouses.

Pray with me:

God, thank You for Your great examples of love. When I did not know You, You loved me enough to save my life and my eternal destination. Through my life, I have witnessed You open doors I could not open, save me from attacks and help me get out of situations that I got myself in, even when I was not honoring You and showing love in return. Help me to use my gratefulness as fuel to love my spouse as You have loved me. There are times when it is difficult because I feel like my needs are being unmet. Strengthen my resolve to love anyway. Transform my heart. Let my desires be to give more than they are to receive. Help me to faithfully wait for the fruit of the right seeds sown into my relationship. Thank You in advance. Amen.

Declaration

I will love my spouse in every season, especially the harder ones, continually seeking to fulfill their needs and desires. In moments when there are disconnects and discomfort, I will remind myself of their worth and value. I will be disciplined to act on who they are to me and not on what they are or are not doing for me. I believe the fruit of my labor will come to pass. I will reap a harvest in my relationship because I have consistently chosen to honor God and my spouse and love selflessly. No one on this earth can love my spouse better than me, and I will prove that through my selfless giving. I will pay the expense of the past so that we can move forward. Every day, I am maturing in my resolve and discipline to love.

Chapter 8:

Love is not Easily Angered

LOVE IS NOT EASILY ANGERED

Anger is a strong displeasure that drives someone into a warlike demeanor. Usually, the feeling we get when we act out of anger is power and control, but the reality is that it is just the opposite. Not to get too scientific or psychological, but the amygdala is the part of the brain that responds to threats. It is instinctive in that it causes us to act before we have been able to give any thought to the perceived threat. We have no mental control over the bodily response. That is not power over the situation. That is the situation having power over us, but we can learn to develop skills to slow down this response when we are angered. The power we feel is just adrenaline temporarily being released into our bodies. Our muscles tense up; our focuses narrow on the target. We also lose the ability to recall things that are said and done during this episode of anger. With these facts, it is easy to determine that we are not in any sound state of mind to resolve conflict with our significant others when we are angry.

As dreadful as acting in anger can be, love has grace on us as humans. The scriptures teach us that love is not easily angered which is significantly different than saying love is never angered. God is concerned about four significant things when it comes to anger: the ease at which we are angered, the duration of our anger, what we allow ourselves to be angry about, and whether we act out of anger.

Rate Yourself

On a scale of 1 to 5 (1 being rarely angered and 5 being easily angered), how easily are you angered? _____

On a scale of 1 to 5 (1 being angered for a short period and 5 being angry for a long time), what is the duration of time you are usually angry? _____

Choose from one of the five statements concerning what type of things anger you most often.

o I get angry when we allow ourselves to operate outside of the spirit and we miss the mark. (1)

Chapter 8

o I get angry after huge disappointments or after I have been let down one too many times. (2)

o I get angry when I am confronted in the wrong way. (3)

o I get angry when I must deal with things that should be understood and is common sense. (4)

o I get mad when I must do things like repeat myself, wait longer than necessary or just when I am not in the best of moods already. (5)

Choose from one of the five statements concerning what you usually do when you are angered.

o I take a moment to process why I am angry and try to communicate it once I've moved pass the emotions. (1)

o I shut down so that I do not get enraged to the point I want to become combative. I work to move past the anger. (2)

o I let it be known that I am angry. Usually, my tone and volume give evidence of it. (3)

o I usually confront them for making me angry which may include telling them what I think about them in the moment. This can usually escalate the argument. (4)

o I usually become confrontational with physical appearances of anger (frowning, hard breathes, slamming doors, etc.). The volume of my voice usually increases significantly.

Take a moment to tally up the points from your self-assessment. Below, you can see what your anger rating is.

(4 – 7): You have a good level of control over anger. You are likely to successfully navigate through offenses and consider the value of your mate through the process.

(8 – 11): Your anger is not over-bearing. At times, you may find yourself needing to apologize for something said in your anger or revisit a conversation to work on an actual resolution.

(12 – 15): Your anger should be of concern. It is hindering the progression and overall intimacy in your relationship.

(16 – 20): You are in danger of regrettably destroying your relationship. When you're angered, it controls what you say and do.

I hope you were as honest as possible with your self-assessment. For greater clarity, ask your spouse to rate you in these areas. If you need a third opinion, also ask a reliable friend to rate you as well.

What Did You Do

It is not uncommon to respond negatively to offenses or other things that anger us. In our human nature, we are less likely to respond positively when someone has upset us. I can recall too many occasions when I yelled or insulted someone in my anger. If I am being transparent, when I was even younger, I can remember even punching walls and inanimate objects in my anger. I punched a steel door, once! Thank God my wife never has seen that side of me before! I want you to take a trip down memory lane for a moment. I want you to think about a few events in life when someone or something made you angry. I want you to write down what happened to you on one side, and on the other side, I want you to write down how you responded.

What happened to you?	How did you respond?
1.	
2.	
3.	

Chapter 8

4.	

    I'm sure you may have experienced some serious offenses throughout your life. Challenging ones, too. From the table you have filled out, I want you to do something. I want you to cover the left side and read out loud what you wrote on the right side. Do you believe what you read accurately describes the type of person you are? Are these things that you desire to be defined by? I don't know what you wrote down, but if your answer was no to either of these questions, know that the left side of the table does speak to those people and who they are, but the right side speaks to who we are exclusive of what was written on the left side. If we react in anger in ways we do not desire, we must be mindful that it is an internal and not an external source of those reactions. Even if somebody hurt us deeply, it isn't the hurt but the unforgiveness that drives us to rage. Even with the process of forgiveness, it takes time to get over the hurt. In the meantime, we must be aware of our triggers and have a strategy to avoid or deescalate them when they arrive.

Activity
All Guns on Safety

Think about typical things that usually make you angry. Make a list of them and ask your spouse to do the same. Share your lists with each other. Give whatever clarity you can about why those things make you angry. Make a pact that these areas are off limits. If you have things that take you over during disagreements, then those things should be avoided. It does not mean that you do not address concerns. It means you agree to pursue healthier ways of presenting them and resolving them. Of course, we are human. Make an agreement with each that if you "violate" the pact, you will apologize and help the other calm down. For example, my wife gets upset when I talk over her (like many people would). I am making efforts to avoid doing this or at least to immediately apologize once I have and let her continue to speak.

    Just because we have a right to be angry does not make it right to be angry. We may not run and grab divorce papers every time the other acts in anger. However, the fact that nothing severe happened should be considered to be grace or even to be the calm before a mightier storm. Managing anger is a discipline. It is safer and healthier to be disciplined than to be driven by magical moments evolving out of chaos, expecting at the end of all of the yelling and the arguing there will be hugs and kisses. Surely, it can happen, but I wouldn't rely on it.

Remember these key practical things you can do if you struggle with anger:

- Get help – don't be too embarrassed or prideful to find anger management classes and other resources.
- Pray as you listen. Meditate on God being present to keep your spirit as you engage in difficult conversations.
- Give yourself space. Nothing is wrong with taking a moment to find peace before having difficult conversations or following an offense.

Pray with me:

Heavenly Father, keep my spirit so that anger does not destroy the things I value. Strengthen my spirit to not operate in anger but to honor and value others in my conversations. Help me to be quick to forgive offenses and wise to seek understanding during confusion. Help me repair the damage done by previous acts of anger. Redeem the time that has been lost and mend the relationships. Amen.

Declaration

I will not be driven or dominated by anger. I will honor and respect others enough to withhold the severity of my anger when I am disappointed or upset. I will communicate with my spouse with love, compassion and respect. I will operate with self-control. I will pray and meditate on the love of God to enable me to extend it to my loved ones when I am let down or hurt. I will take the initiative to resolve the conflict in my life. I will not seek revenge but reconciliation in my relationships.

Chapter 9:

It Keeps No Record of Wrongs

Chapter 9
IT KEEPS NO RECORD OF WRONGS

What do we gain when people "get what they deserve" after wronging us? Many of us never let it go until "the score is settled." What do we believe "getting away with it" communicates to us? That it is unfair? That our feelings or lives are not valued if they don't answer for their wrongs? How do we define people or remember people by their wrongs, yet we work to move forward in life omitting or overlooking our own wrongs? Is that fair? Are we serving the feelings that emerged from the wrongs rather than a greater sense of character and identity? Recall from the story of Joseph and his brothers, when they thought he would serve vengeance upon them, as they remembered all that they had done to him, his response was simply, "Don't be afraid. Am I in the place of God? You intended to harm me, but God intended it for good to accomplish what is now being done, the saving of many lives (Genesis 50:19)." Are you and I in the place of God? Are our feelings and hurts in the place of God? Of course, they shouldn't be if they are. Yes, our identities and our feelings matter, but they should have no authority over how we treat each other. God's commandments do – all for a good reason.

More Honesty

Be honest. In your relationship, what position have you placed yourself in when you are wronged? Are you positioning yourself to be the judge of your loved one? The punisher? The victim? The hero? Write down your normal response to wrongs. Describe how that role matures or changes when the wrong is more severe.

_____
_____
_____
_____
_____
_____
_____

Chapter 9

Once Upon a Time...

Everybody likes a good story whether we are reading it, watching it unfold in a movie or listening to someone talk about an event of his/her life. We are either entertained by great victories or great adversities. I've recalled many times people compete over who is struggling the most or who has endured more pain. Someone may mention they went a week without electricity which compels the next to mention they had to sleep in their vehicle for a few days. Are we crying out for sympathy or bragging rights? Does either make sense? Maybe it is because we feel like we have a stronger argument on the adversity end of our story than we do the victory side. Maybe our victories seem too "normal" to retell, so it is not a part of our story when we tell it. Could this be the same reason we mention our problems in our relationship more often than just saying we are getting along. Getting along everyday seems "too normal." There is no entertainment or energy in the thought.

How have you generally told the story of your relationship in the past? What have you recorded and represented when it is spoken of? When you think about your life/marriage/children, what is the first thing you recall? Most importantly, what story do you tell yourself?

_____
_____
_____
_____
_____
_____
_____
_____

The Best Storytellers

As I look back on some of the most amazing writers, reporters and storytellers, it isn't the story itself that makes the story worth hearing. It is how the person is telling the story: the energy an expression used, the visual details that are placed in the story, and the confidence that the story is worth being told. You may believe that the wrongs of your relationship are worth the focus, but I challenge you to retell what is going right with greater energy, paying attention to the details and with the confidence that the good things are worth being told.

I want to give you an opportunity to tell the story of your relationship in a new, exciting way. Recall any good moment in your relationship, small or big. Recall the visuals: what you smelled and any other thing that appeals to any of our five senses. Do not write it down reluctantly, but like the story is worth being told. You can write about the time you scrambled eggs together. Nothing is too small, too normal or too insignificant. Have fun with this one and feel free to share it with your mate.

_____

_____

_____

_____

_____

_____

_____

_____

_____

_____

_____

_____

_____

_____

Boulders vs. Stepping Stones

Many of us do not tap into our creativity. We take things as they traditionally have been presented to us. Logic and pattern are our boundaries. We will only climb

Chapter 9

things that were designed to be climbed: ladders and stairs. The reality is that there are so many other objects that can assist in elevating us: chairs, other people, and even boulders. Most of us would probably prefer an escalator or an elevator, but we should not limit our elevation to these options. God is a creative God. He wastes nothing in our lives. The bible tells us that "all things work together [as a plan] for the good of those who love God, to those who are called according to His plan and purpose" (Romans 8:28). Every time I see the reference of loving God, I now think about the scripture that says, "The person who has My commandments and keeps them is the one who [really] loves Me… (John 14:21)". I believe it is good to ask ourselves if we intend to and practice keeping God's commandments before zealously claiming that we love Him. It is no doubt that God has a plan and a purpose for all our lives, and if we would love Him by following His commandments, we will see the good come out of everything in our lives.

Joseph recognized this in the wrongs of his brothers and he told them, "…You intended to harm me, but God intended it for good to accomplish what is now being done, the saving of many lives" (Genesis 50:19). He knew they meant to harm him. He also understood that God used his enslavement as a creative way to introduce him to Pharaoh, who made him second in command. Joseph not only forgave his ill-intending brothers, but he also took care of them. Instead of seeking revenge, he acknowledged the purpose behind the wrong. If he had remained bitter and unforgiving, he could not have lived out the purpose that God was ultimately setting him up to do.

Your Turn: It Burned but It is Better

Identify a wrong you endured in your relationship. How has or how can God use that to shape you and/or your relationship? Keep in mind, it is possible not to understand how it is being used for good but know that God is working on it. Joseph could not have predicted enslavement and a prison sentence would elevate him to next in command to the Pharaoh. I never knew dealing with my wife's opportunities would help me work on true selflessness. We never knew our faults would help us live by a truer, unconditional love.

_____

_____

_____

_____

Let's Not Get Too Literal

So, what does keeping a record of wrongs look like? Is it journaling and recording dates every time your loved one offends you? Yes, it is. I have met some people who committed to doing this so that they would have stronger arguments the next time they would feud with one another. They both recognized that it was unhealthy for their relationship and themselves as people. We can put so much effort into winning a battle that we lose the war. Is it worth it to win an argument and lose the love of your life?

They made literal records of their wrongs, but we don't always make literal records of wrongs in our relationships. However, just as it is with literal records, we can put the energy into winning the battle and end up losing our relationships in the process. Before we go into other ways to take record, let's look at some other reasons we do it. Not all of us simple want to win an argument. The reality is that when we are wronged or hurt there is an instinct that makes note of the offense so that we avoid impeding danger in the future. The amygdala in our brains does the work for us. Yes, it is our very nature to keep record, yet God instructs us not to do so in the name of love! This is just a reminder that God has given us instructions that are walked out in the spirit and not in the flesh, which means that we depend on our relationship with Him to accomplish these things and not our own might or will.

So, to give a general statement of what records look like, it means to replay and interact with someone on the accords of previous faults. "She overspent so she can never use the debit cards again." "He refused to listen to me, so I am never talking about my concerns again." We keep record when we dictate how the future will play out by pinpointing a similar failure in the past. Listen, we are setting ourselves up for failure when we believe our relationships, spouses and ourselves are defined by a single moment in the past and that we cannot improve. The aim is to not live in the past and to treat each new moment as an opportunity to be better. Lastly, one of the worst ways we keep record is when we replay the negative moments over and over in our brain during the idle time of our day, literally like a spinning record. Change the song! We cannot be our best when we live in the negative as a default.

Recognize and Replace

Chapter 9

In a moment, I want you to recognize any past wrong you have recorded in any type of way: written, replayed in your mind as a default, or used to define your spouse in critical moments. After you have recognized it, I want you to replace that record with either a record of the past that counters that thought or a statement of hope and belief for the future.

Example:
Record: When I asked her to come out to support an important event, she didn't which means she doesn't care about my dreams.
Replace: There have been many times she has come out to watch me perform. She may not show the enthusiasm I desire, but she makes the sacrifice of time to support.
Or
Replace: My wife and I are learning how to balance time and value each other's interests. As I learn to support her, she will also learn to support me.

Record: _____
_____
_____

Replace: _____
_____
_____

Record: _____
_____
_____

Replace: _____
_____
_____

Record: _____
_____
_____

Replace: _____

Record: _____

_____

_____

Replace: _____

_____

_____

Forgiveness – Facing the Facts

For those of us who are hurt, forgiveness can be the last thing we want to hear or talk about. It does not readily seem to change our circumstances or improve our situations. We all like to be forgiven, but we do not enjoy offering the forgiveness. Even though it may seem like forgiveness shouldn't be a priority to some, it is our responsibility to focus on forgiveness. It is one of the things we can do for ourselves. So, let's look at some facts concerning forgiveness.

Fact #1: Forgiveness is not earned, it is transferred. If you do not forgive, God will not forgive you. You will carry the weight of your own sins and shortcomings due to your lack of forgiveness. You will not live in peace.

If you forgive others their trespasses [their reckless and willful sins], your heavenly Father will also forgive you. But if you do not forgive others [nurturing your hurt and anger with the result that it interferes with your relationship with God], then your Father will not forgive your trespasses. ~ Matthew 6:14-15

Complete this sentence: I will continually forgive _____, not because he/she has earned it but because I love him/her, and I will show them the same grace and compassion that God has shown and will continue to show me all the years of my life.

Fact #2: Forgiveness is a healer. Unforgiveness is a killer.

He who covers and forgives an offense seeks love, but he who repeats or gossips about a matter separates intimate friends. ~Proverbs 17:9

Chapter 9

Answer this question: What do you desire for your relationship? Will forgiveness or unforgiveness direct you towards that desire? If unforgiveness will, then how? If forgiveness will, then how? What can you do to be intentional about going towards the direction of your desires for your relationship?

_____
_____
_____
_____
_____
_____
_____
_____
_____
_____
_____

Dismember Them

Did this workbook just go dark? Not at all. If you recall from the text of the book and the bible, the scripture tells us in Psalms 103:12

As far as the east is from the west, so far has He removed our transgressions from us.

The children of Israel were not pure when they made this statement. It wasn't that they would not sin in the future, either. God let the past be the past and decided to move forward after the children of Israel renewed their hearts with God. In forgiving our mates, we let the past be the past and walk forward with them as they renew their hearts and walk with us.

> **Activity**
> *Dismemberment*
>
> Whatever you have been holding on to in your relationship and towards your significant other, I want you to take out a sheet of paper. Write your spouse's name in the middle of the paper. Write out each hurt and grudge you have held on to. When you are done, take a good look at the paper. That is how you have viewed and consequentially treated them. Now, I want you to either scratch out or cut out each hurt and offense. As you do so, pray and ask God to help you separate them from their offenses in your heart. Once you have removed all of them, take another look at the paper. This paper now symbolizes the hurt and damage they have walked in due to your unforgiveness. Now, pray and ask God to help you mend the brokenness that may exist in your relationship.

Current Events

Possibly, throughout this discussion and these activities, you may have thought of some things that are still going on in the present. First, let's be clear. Keeping no record of wrongs does not mean we do not do our parts in promoting the health and welfare of our relationships. Part of that promoting is addressing the opportunities we see in ourselves and our mates. Seek God in prayer to see what offenses are insignificant and should be overlooked and which ones need a conversation had in love to discuss the concerns and potential solutions. You may discover that clothes being left on the floor is not worth the same energy as using hateful words.

However, it should be noted that healing, correction and growth are part of a process. Be encouraged to even move pass what happened yesterday or even what happened two hours ago. Forgiveness is a continual commitment, just as much as we need it from God.

Then Peter came to Him and asked, "Lord, how many times will my brother sin against me and I will forgive him and let it go? Up to seven times?" Jesus answered him, "I say to you, not up to seven times, but seventy times seven." ~Matthew 18:21-22

So, create a tally sheet and... I'm just kidding. Jesus was not giving a literal number. Who wants to count 490 sins? How could you keep up? The answer is that we are not supposed to keep up. As often as our loved ones sin against us, forgive. Can you imagine what our tallies would look like right now if God was keeping count? Again, this does not mean we get walked on or that we do not address the issues and work towards renewal. It means we don't allow the hurt or the natural desire to avoid hurt to give anger and

Chapter 9

bitterness permission to further direct our lives and draw us away from God and the people we have commissioned to love.

Pray with me:

Lord, help me destroy the record of offenses. I acknowledge how unworthy I am of Your forgiveness. I acknowledge the magnitude of Your grace, mercy and love towards me. Strengthen me to offer that same love towards others, especially my spouse. I cannot imagine living life without Your forgiveness, and I do not desire to live that way. I believe Your commandments are what are best for me. Help me to follow them, even when my nature wars against them. Thank You for Your constant example. Amen.

Declaration

I will not define my significant other by his/her mistakes and offenses. I believe in the healing process of forgiveness. Nothing will separate me from the love of God found in Christ, and I will use that inseparable love to strengthen and renew my relationship. I have the character and virtue of a true believer. I can overcome what is natural to man to do what is spiritual. I am not a victim. We are more than conquerors. I will overlook the offenses and cover my spouse in love. We will walk the road to healing together. Every day, I will seek to see my significant other as God sees them and not as the sum of the hurts I have endured. We will live in peace because of it.

Chapter 10:

Love Does Not Delight in Evil, But Rejoices with the Truth

Chapter 10
LOVE DOES NOT DELIGHT IN EVIL BUT REJOICES WITH THE TRUTH

Four letter words! Yikes! Some of us let them roll right off the tongue. Others among us gasp as soon as we hear one. What about the four-letter word *evil*? None of us want to be associated with that word. Remember, however, that it is not the Boogieman or Count Dracula that we are referring to as evil. Evil is simply anything morally wrong or bad. If we are honest with ourselves, we all have been evil at some point and in some act.

Since all have sinned and continually fall short of the glory of God... ~Romans 3:23

That is right. We have sinned and will continually sin as long as we are wrapped in this flesh and breath on this side of life. You know what? Even though I will continually sin throughout this life, I do not have to delight in it. I can recognize it, confess it, and continue to press towards a higher mark in my spirituality and devotion to God through my actions. I can constantly thank God for His grace and His ultimate sacrifice that He has offered me through undeserving salvation, but I do not have to abuse that grace.

Here is the kicker. We may not want to admit it, but evil feels good. Doesn't it? To our flesh, right? I mean, what does the flesh desire? For those of us who had sex before marriage, it felt good, didn't it? When we cursed out the person that upset us, laughed at someone who has been talked about badly, saw the demise of an enemy, or had so many drinks that the time escaped us, it felt good. All of it is sin, though. Sin promises us something of value, but to the spirit, it only offers guilt and shame. Of course, our flesh trusts more in evil than it does good. Evil offers power, control, pleasure, respect and confidence. Everything that God asks us to surrender to Him, the flesh persuades us to keep it. Unfortunately, these decisions affect our attitudes and responses in our relationships.

Trusting Shadows

Where have you trusted in evil ways for yourself? To get a promotion? To get in a relationship? To win an argument?

_____
_____
_____
_____
_____

What do you know is *wrong* to do that you still find yourself doing? Call it evil and turn away from it.

_____
_____
_____
_____
_____

The Mirage

Society has a way of weighing *evil* deeds. We obviously look at murder differently than lying on taxes. We look at stealing differently than slandering a name. There is the law of the land that determines the extremity of illegal sin and there is the unspoken social law for everything else that isn't necessarily illegal. The most important determinant in our actions, however, is our own hearts. Regardless if man says it is or isn't okay, we are governed by our own hearts. Some of us will portray to trust God and His ways to save face, but our hearts trust in our own minds and methods which are usually contradictory to God's and ultimately are sin. Note this: It isn't sin just because it disagrees with God. It is sin because God knows the right way to do things, so by default, the opposite is the wrong way – the morally wrong way, which is evil. In critical situations, many give God's ways as advice, but when we face them ourselves, we are reluctant to turn to His ways. Why is that?

Chapter 10

Take a moment to write out your thoughts on this.

_____
_____
_____
_____

That Just Doesn't Work

If we look at our relationships, the most common time we find ourselves tempted to delight in evil is when our spouses have offended or upset us. In this moment, the evil offers us revenge, justice or simply the pleasure of expressing our emotions in the moment. We will name call, judge, or say other hurtful things. We will remain distant and cold. Some of us even shut off connection and communication completely. The evil presents itself as a weapon of defense, but God already offered us a weapon in His word and through kindness. Here's the question: do you want to punish your mate, or do you want them to be disciplined – to learn how to handle the situation better next time?

Have you ever "punished" your mate for an offense? What was the outcome?

_____
_____
_____
_____

Some of us may feel gratification in that the punishment led us to get our way, but did the punishment draw us closer? Do we feel as connected to them as before, if not more? Do they further understand our love for them after the moment has passed? If you are looking to serve yourself in a relationship, you are likely to lose. If you will make sacrifices for love's sake, you are likely to save your relationship and yourself in the process. When somebody has hurt us, consequences are not a bad thing, but the goal should still be reconciliation. The challenge is that most of us do not have these consequences built into our relationships.

Activity
Justifiably So

A few offenses are listed below. Sit with your spouse and determine what are rightful consequences to the offense. You may be surprised how awkward the conversation will be or how uncertain you are about what the consequences should be because we usually impulsively respond. Talk about it, and when you have agreed, write it down here.

Raising your voice/Cursing at your mate/Name calling: _____
_____
_____
_____

Overspending the money: _____
_____
_____
_____

Not carrying your weight around the house: _____
_____
_____
_____

Define *serious offenses* and the consequences: _____
_____
_____

Not fulfilling your word given: _____
_____
_____

Chapter 10

As you complete the activity, it is doubtful that you will decide to not speak to each other or to return the offense, but without an agreement and by acting on emotion and impulse, these become the designated consequences, but they are not healthy consequences. Our consequences should be geared towards recognizing the wrong and mending from the offense. Anything else serves our pride and emotions. Anything else will not benefit us individually or relationally. For major offenses, consider help such as seeking counsel or fasting and praying together. Do not run to ideas of divorce or other things that primarily focus on the hurt that would be created from the offense. Have a plan that enables you to discover a path to reconciliation.

Many of us fear having agreed on paths to take for major offenses that seem to invalidate our hurt and feelings when these things have happened. Some of us may even fear that our mates will abuse the system by knowing we are agreeing to work with them in the event something extremely undesirable happens. These are understood concerns. There is no perfect system. These things may not prevent tragedy, but it is a step in the right direction to protect the health of our relationships. The good thing about it is that we can take it even a step further. We can establish some safeguards to approach these major offenses before they even happen or before they get out of hand. One part of trusting our mates to not do extremely damaging things in our relationship is to be trustworthy enough ourselves that they feel safe and secure coming to us when they are being challenged in these areas. You may not want them to cheat on you, but are you selfless and considerate enough for them to come to you and tell you that someone is making them feel more desirable than you currently are? If you would rather focus on your disappointment in that moment, then you have set your own mate up for failure. Expecting them to just deal with it or to feel wrong for having the temptation without resolving the gap that opened the temptation isn't a sound approach, and it doesn't draw you closer. Yes, the conversation may be uncomfortable, but it is more than worth having. Set some boundaries on the delivery of the conversation, pray, and talk it out.

LOVE DOES NOT DELIGHT IN EVIL BUT REJOICES WITH THE TRUTH

Activity
Proactive Measures

For the three major offenses listed below, list some things you would invite your mate to do before they give in to the desire to commit the act. Also, write out what you agree to do in support of helping them overcome the unwanted desires.

Cheating or seeking the flattery, attention or support of someone else: _____

_____

_____

_____

_____

Using drugs or drinking alcohol in excess (Returning or for the first time): _____

_____

_____

_____

_____

Gambling with needed funds or making extreme big purchases: _____

_____

_____

_____

_____

Chapter 10

The Truth of the Matter

The valued friends of mine and their names will remain anonymous, but I do have to address the ideas surrounding the reality of what is and what isn't – "my truth." My truth is deemed to be what I live in, my circumstances, my issues, my opportunities, my enemies, my friends and my life, as I see it. You may see things differently, but my truth is my truth. Whereas "my truth" and "your truth" should be heard and understood, we must humbly admit that our truths simply lack the depth of understanding and objectivity to define life, including our own lives. It doesn't mean that our feelings, desires, thoughts and ideas do not matter. It means there is a greater, more dominant, more reliable source of truth – God's word. I must learn to trust God enough to accept that any part of my truth that disagrees with His truth is simply not true. God says that His word will never come back to Him void – not fulfilling what He sent it out to do (Isaiah 55:11). The bible also instructs us not to rely on our own understanding, but in all our ways, acknowledge God (Proverbs 3:5-6). Our truths may conflict with God's on occasion. His trumps ours.

Our love desires to trust in God's word, His commands and His promises – the truth. Our flesh trusts in our feelings and mindsets. It trusts in our limited experiences and formulized opinions. It trusts in our eyes and not our faith. These are not truths but are static pictures of life and jaded views of a greater story being told. Know that there are so many things fighting against God's truth. There are many things on the inside of us that makes us reject the good news God offers us – that we can do all things through Christ who strengthens us (Philippians 4:13) and so many other truths God delivers us. Know this, disagreeing with the fact that God calls you great and mighty in the land (Psalm 112:2) or that you are the apple of his eye (Zechariah 2:8) doesn't make you humble. It means you deny His truth. I am not judging you for it. In the vein of self-worth and confidence, I have warred against what God says about me on many occasions. The reality is that it is simply a struggle sometimes to receive what He says about us, but it should still be our goal – not something we fight against.

Peter's Denial – Upon the persecution of Jesus, Peter denied three times knowing Jesus. He feared for his own life and did not want to be subject to the same scrutiny and peril as Jesus was being faced with. Many elements simply attack our desires to trust and stand with God.

LOVE DOES NOT DELIGHT IN EVIL BUT REJOICES WITH THE TRUTH

What have you disagreed with God about, and what factors have caused you to disagree?

_____

_____

_____

_____

_____

Choose This Day

When Joshua took on the task of completing the mission of leading the children of Israel to the promised land, some of the followers were still wanting to assimilate with other teachings and gods. Joshua told them to choose, this day, whom they would serve (Joshua 24: 14-15). Jesus informed us that we cannot serve two masters (Matthew 6:24). The reality is that we cannot live in God's truth and a lie, simultaneously. We must remove the lie to receive the truth. In fact, we cannot even receive greater application of God's truth if, in a large capacity, we are doubting or ready to reject it.

But he must ask [for wisdom] in faith, without doubting [God's willingness to help], for the one who doubts is like a billowing surge of the sea that is blown about and tossed by the wind. For such a person ought not to think or expect that he will receive anything [at all] from the Lord, being a double-minded man, unstable and restless in all his ways [in everything he thinks, feels, or decides]. ~ James 1:6-8

Where's the Lie – Take a moment to journal any thought, idea or inner vow that has been conflicting with the type of person God is commissioning you to be or that has challenged the actions you should be taking to promote a healthier relationship. Write down any evil thoughts that have haunted your mindset, choices and actions. Pray on these things and seek scriptures that speak against these things and offer more sound perspectives and instructions for you concerning these areas of focus.

Chapter 10

_____

_____

_____

_____

_____

_____

We do not have to be fearful of living in the truth of God. Love by the power of God, experiences victory. It is a truth we should live in with conviction and tenacity. Following God means to obey His commandments and to learn to live as He has designated us to live: abundantly, with self-control, with a pure heart and free from the entanglement of sin. There is a great evil that wars against this that either attempts to offer similar things through unsound methods or that attempts to enslave us through shame and image bashings. Stand on what God says about you when these things come to tempt or attack.

Pray with me:

Heavenly Father help me to seek the truth that You have provided me through Your word. Discipline me to stand on your word when the world and circumstances tempt me to do otherwise. Guide me to live out Your truth through my choices and actions, especially as they relate to what You say about my relationship. Reveal the truth about my mate. Reveal the truth about me. Reveal the truth concerning what You desire for my relationship. Help me to trust it simply because You spoke it. In Jesus' name I pray. Amen.

Declaration

I am casting down all things that exalts itself above God's word. I will live by the word and truth of God. I cast out my own limited perspectives to acknowledge and live by the sound and just wisdom of God. I believe that God knows what is best for my life and those around me. I will believe what God says about the people around me, especially

LOVE DOES NOT DELIGHT IN EVIL BUT REJOICES WITH THE TRUTH

my mate. I will count those things that God calls a blessing as a blessing. I will count those things that God calls a curse a curse. I believe that God uses all things to work for my benefit and not my demise. I yield my thoughts, feelings and attitudes to His truth for my life. Anything that contradicts what God says about me and my life is a lie, and I will not live in a lie. I will continually seek the truth of God and turn away from the evil things that feed my flesh.

Chapter 11:

Love Always Protects

LOVE ALWAYS PROTECTS

If you have ever attended a marriage class or conference, you may have heard them say, "Marriages are under attack" or "The devil does not want you to have a good marriage." If you attend a class regularly, these statements may have become a norm to the point you are numb to them, but they are as true the hundredth time you've heard them as they were the first time. There is a real threat to EVERY marriage, including yours. Do not take it lightly. If you desire to honor God with your relationship, you are even higher on the radar for an attack.

Prior to writing *What Is Love*, a good friend of mine and I talked about all that we have learned on our journey to become better men, husbands and fathers. We talked about the lack of connection and resources that were available to us before we made the mistakes we made and before we got deep into our struggles. We both share a desire to reach out and help others. Surely enough, as we geared up to do just that, both of our marriages went under attack, intensely paralyzing our efforts to do anything but try to deal with the war at home. We spent the remaining year digging our heels in to keep our marriages together and moving forward. Most of the time, it was due to confusion or a relapse of feelings and emotions, but the energy was severe enough to cause stress, anxiety and even depression.

You may be wondering what happened when I finally decided to write the book or later create this workbook. Did I finally find a peaceful window to focus? Nope. That's right. As I write these words, my marriage is currently being attacked again with the same confusion, relapse of hurt and exhaustive energy. This time around, while I am yet fighting the war that is, I am also pushing forward to help others along the way. We must break the cycle rather wait for the cycle to break for us. We must pass whatever tests God is allowing. We must continue to protect what is valuable to us. If there are complications in your marriage, you may very well be under attack. Be of good cheer, just as I know my wife and I will come out of this moment, I believe you and your mate will, too. The key is to not define you, your spouse or your relationships by your problems, mistakes, or faults. Define you, your spouse and your relationship by the fact that you have the capacity to overcome all of your faults and challenges. Protect what you believe in.

Chapter 11

Call It Out

In what ways has the enemy attacked your marriage?

_____

_____

_____

_____

_____

_____

Join with your spouse and pray over those areas. Look at the areas that the devil has attacked and view it as evidence that these areas have value and that the value is greater than the attack on it.

It's Chess, Not Checkers

As discussed in the book, your marriage isn't under attack just because the devil and the world doesn't want you to be happy. The devil is after your children and your children's children. It is understanding the principal of reaping and sowing. Bad seeds yield bad fruit. The bible confirms this (Galatians 6:7). There are a few tactics the devil uses to create bad seeds. It has been proven that divorce is a mental and spiritual form of death, if not for the actual espoused couple, but for their children. However, the devil does not necessarily have to get you to divorce. If he can successfully fill the home with resentment, hate, anger and selfishness, those elements will be perpetuated in the relationships of your children. The danger in that is that the Spirit of God cannot operate in resentment, hate, anger and selfishness.

The danger is that the devil doesn't physically walk in our doors and raise hell. He doesn't speak in an apparent demonic voice which would freak us all out. He whispers. He asks questions. He insights temptation. If he can successfully gel his words with ours, if he can make what he desires and what we desire become one, and if he can successfully label our mates as the enemy and hide in the background, he can destroy our marriages and our legacy. So, instead of trying to figure out what the devil is up to, we can simply examine our own thoughts and actions.

Who are you producing fruit for in your thoughts and actions? The devil or God? Account for all your actions. If there is some part of you that is producing bad fruit, confess it here.

_____

_____

_____

_____

_____

_____

_____

The Triple Threat – Satan, The World, Our Flesh

It is important to be aware of the triple threat against your relationships and the overall quality of life. It is also important to understand their tactics for attacking to be able to properly and effectively use counteractive and preventative measures. The devil appeals to fulfill a need or strong desire through his own methods that entice you to knowingly or unknowingly serve him. He ignites the areas we are tempted in: lust, pride or idolatry. He makes these things appear as just and that we are entitled to act out these desires whether it be as a method of revenge, an effort to "take care of self," or simply because "the good outweighs the bad" in our choices. Be warned, the bible instructs us to "… not give the devil an opportunity [to lead you into sin by holding a grudge, or nurturing anger, or harboring resentment, or cultivating bitterness]" (Ephesians 4:27).

The world seeks rebellion towards God, seeking everything God has promised without following His commands to receive them. In this, the world tempts us to utilize

Chapter 11

its methods of having a good relationship and ignore the foundations God has built to ensure healthy relationships. The world uses strong words, imagery and "flashy lights" to make its way appear more attractive and promising. Again, the bible says, "You adulteresses [disloyal sinners – flirting with the world and breaking your vow to God]! Do you not know that being the world's friend [that is, loving the things of the world] is being God's enemy? So whoever chooses to be a friend of the world makes himself an enemy of God" (James 4:4). Realize that, when we choose the ways of this world, we choose to rebel against God. I know it may seem extreme to say. Of course, the world would love to minimize it so that you would be more willing to side with it. Know that it matters to God for you to knowingly choose the world over Him.

Our flesh desires to carry out all of its vices at the expense of our relationship with God and others:

For the flesh desires what is contrary to the Spirit, and the Spirit what is contrary to the flesh. They are in conflict with each other, so that you are not to do whatever you want. But if you are led by the Spirit, you are not under the law. The acts of the flesh are obvious: sexual immorality, impurity and debauchery; idolatry and witchcraft; hatred, discord, jealousy, fits of rage, selfish ambition, dissensions, factions and envy; drunkenness, orgies and the like. I warn you, as I did before, that those who live like this will not inherit the kingdom of God. ~Galatians 5:17-21

Quickly recognize that allowing any one of these acts to lead your choices in life are from the wrong source. They are an attack on you, your relationship with God and your relationship with others. The only reward is the flesh being made stronger in your life, only to dominate your future choices on a larger scale. That's not really a reward at all. Remember, the wages (reward) for sin is death (Romans 6:23).

Don't minimize the effects of these threats. Realize that the unwillingness to follow God's ways is an indicator of pride or perhaps fear, two things that shouldn't govern our lives and relationships. It may seem difficult to turn away from these things, but it is beneficial to your soul and your relationships.

The Divorce

Before your marriage ends in divorce, we need to divorce our relationships with Satan, the world and our flesh, so let's get started!

I, _____, in the presence of God, in honor of my family and the legacy I desire to live out, and in response to my desire to love my spouse and create a healthy, secure relationship, do solemnly and sincerely disavow my relationships with Satan, the world and my flesh. They will no longer dominate my desires, thoughts and actions. I will no longer rely on them for my sense of value, respect, fulfillment or protection.

I, _____, solemnly and sincerely, promise to navigate my life using the Word of God as my guide. I am marrying my heart to the heart of God. My choices and my thoughts will be filtered through the Spirit. I will devote myself to be an accurate representative of God on earth.

I, _____, make this pledge without reluctance but through a commitment to trust God at His word and with the hope and faith of the promises found in His word.

Signature: _____

Rules for Engagement – How to Protect

In the book *What Is Love*, we discussed four methods of protection: attack, defend, cover and flee. All of them are needed for every relationship. Below, you are going to create your battle plan for each of these areas.

Attack – to set upon in a forceful, violent, hostile, or aggressive way.

We can recall that the way we spiritually attack is through the word of God. As the definition of attack indicates, this should not be done lightly or without true power. Murmuring a scripture without conviction may not do the trick. In this section, you will itemize specific spiritual things you want to attack and search the word of God to find scriptures that deal with that area. If you are not a bible scholar, you can use the internet to look up suggestions. For example, if I wanted to attack depression in my home, I could look up "scriptures that help battle depression."

Chapter 11

What are you attacking? _____

_____

What scripture did you find to declare over this area? _____

_____

_____

What is another thing you are attacking? _____

_____

What scripture did you find to declare over this area? _____

_____

_____

Defend – to support in the face of criticism; prove the validity of by answering arguments and questions put by a committee of specialist.

We learn in the bible that Satan is a specialist at accusing us day in and day out before God (Revelations 12:10). Unfortunately, he is not only accusing us before God. He also accuses our spouses before us, constantly trying to reveal their unworthiness and inadequacies. The danger is, once we agree, we can no longer differentiate his accusations from our very own thoughts. However, just like Jesus defends us before God, we should respond in defense to the accusations against our spouses. Now, you may not know whether it has been the devil or your own mind that has brought down the worth of your mate. It will be healthy to defend these arguments by replacing the thoughts with statements that build your spouse up. For example, if I believed that my wife was inconsiderate. I would step in defense and say that she loves me and is concerned with my well-being. Then, I would bring to my own memory at least one moment where her actions confirmed this statement. So, give it a go here.

Accusation: _____

_____

Defending statement: _____

_____

Evidence: _____

_____

Accusation: _____

_____

Defending statement: _____

_____

Evidence: _____

_____

Accusation: _____

_____

Defending statement: _____

_____

Evidence: _____

_____

Cover – to take temporary charge of or responsibility for in place of another.

I bet, in the defend section, some of you may have been thinking "But my spouse does have REAL issues that I have to deal with." I absolutely do not disagree with you. There are things I must "deal with" from my wife, but there are also things that she must deal with from me. There is no measurement surrounding who must deal more. If we are focusing on having a healthy relationship, it is fruitless to attempt to answer this question anyway. I would rather spend energy believing in the growth and maturity in

Chapter 11

that area and partnering with her thereby sharing some of the responsibility until that day is realized. For example, my wife may not actively engage in dialogue about her concerns until they fester leading her to seemingly attack me. I can harbor over the felt disrespect or I can believe she will begin to feel safe enough to have those conversations before an eruption. In the meantime, I will initiate conversations around things that may concern her, and when she explodes, I will work to maintain the self-control to give evidence that I still care in those moments instead of pointing out how offended I am. Be willing to cover matures both of us at the same time, so commit to this opportunity.

Spouse's opportunity: _____

_____

_____

What are you believing for them? _____

_____

_____

How will you cover/partner with them? _____

_____

_____

Spouse's opportunity: _____

_____

_____

What are you believing for them? _____

_____

_____

How will you cover/partner with them? _____

Flee – to run away, as from danger or pursuers; take flight

This idea of fleeing has two areas of focus. One thing to note is that not all problems warrant attention; they are just distractions. Oftentimes, we magnify something insignificant to something that implicates something totally unrelated to the situation. Hearing your spouse chew their food may be annoying, but does it really require a full-blown argument? Does it make them less competent as a spouse? With these type of things, we should flee from the temptation to ignite division and disrespect among us. Make a list of things that may cause discomfort and annoyance that is simply not worth the attention aside from polite reminders. Agree to flee away from the temptation of allowing these things to spark feuds in your relationship.

1. _____
2. _____
3. _____
4. _____

The other idea of fleeing is foreseeing real dangers or things that could lead to real dangers and removing yourself from them. If watching certain movies or shows make you fantasize in a lustful way and project on your spouse, you may want to avoid those types of movies. Hopefully, you know by now to avoid pornography, but also know that similar energy can be found in many rated R movies these days. If alcohol makes you more confrontational, if certain friends bring out a negative side of you, or if shopping without a list prompts you to excessively spend, refrain from putting yourself in those positions to damage your relationship. Not all dangers are completely avoidable, but we should keep a healthy distance from those that we are aware of. The things I know I should stay away from I refer to as *triggers* to unwanted behavior and/or temptation. There are tons of triggers that can be found on social media and the internet overall! Write down the things that trigger unwanted behavior or energy in yourself or in your relationship. Unless they are genuinely negative, pessimistic people,

Chapter 11

you may not be able to list your in-laws as one of them, just so you know. That last statement was meant to be humorous.

1. _____

2. _____

3. _____

4. _____

Healing and Maintenance

As already indicated, there is a war against marriage, including yours. In any war, there are always opportunities for injuries. The closer and more effective the healing services, the more likely chance there is for survival. Also, life tends to generate wear and tear throughout the many changing seasons. We also want to have tools and resources to maintain our relationships, even when things aren't broken. There are some popular things that are recommended, and I am going to assign to some of them in this workbook. Not all of them will be readily available, but I suggest seeking out each of these resources.

Scriptures – The word of God offers us peace, strength and joy. When we are willing to stand on them, we can renew our resolve to have great relationships. Read the word. When you find scriptures that personally speak to you and your desires for your relationship, write them here.

Scripture 1: _____

_____

_____

Scripture 2: _____

_____

_____

Scripture 3: _____

_____

_____

Prayer – Never underestimate the power of prayer. Prayer activates our faith and is conversation with God, the most powerful, loving being alive. Knowing that He hears you and will also answer your prayers is a great benefit that should never be taken for granted. Pray regularly, not just when there are concerns. You will find your prayer life evolving through each season. Just remember, He is listening, no matter how you think you sound. He is listening, mainly to your heart.

Accountability Partner – An accountability partner is an invaluable resource – someone who is walking through life with you, possessing similar goals with very similar values and virtues. This person understands what you desire out of life and your relationship. This person values you and holds your actions up against that value that has been assigned to you. This person is concerned more with God's truth and your goals more than they are concerned with your feelings. There is a mutually shared trust. If necessary, this person will argue you down before they allow you to make a mistake or give up. On the other end, yes, they will listen to your heart and just be available to understand and empathize. An accountability partner is not someone who will primarily tell you what they think you want to hear or be fearful of losing the friendship for being honest. For years now, I have talked to my accountability partner almost every day, and it has been life giving. There's a sense of humility because both of us are on our own journey, learning from mistakes and celebrating victories. He has become a great treasure to me, and I appreciate him honoring my devotion to my family and standing in the fight with me. We have both put our friendship on the line to fight for the other person's marriage and family. Again, I cannot urge the importance of this.

Pray and reach out to someone you trust to be an accountability partner. The bible tells us there is a friend that sticks closer than any brother (Proverbs 18:24).

Chapter 11

Mentor – Now, a mentor is someone who has "traveled before you" and has already gained wisdom in the area you seek growth. People have business mentors, parenting mentors, and marriage mentors. This person should be vulnerable to share their tangible experiences with the advice they yield, whether those experiences are good or bad. These people should be sound and stable, especially in the area you seek their wisdom. For longevity, it is necessary that this person demonstrates some true desire to see you successful in the area you seek their wisdom. Without it, you may be reluctant to reach out if you begin to feel like a burden. With that being said, be prepared to reach out more than they reach out to you. Most successful people have very intentional schedules and timelines, and they anticipate you making it a priority to set up the time you need to speak with them, not because they are so important but as evidence that what you are aiming for is important to you.

Counseling – Now, I saved counseling for last, not because it is least important. In fact, it is just as important as all the others mentioned. There is a stigma concerning counseling that I hope you do not operate in. Counseling is not for damaged people or relationships. It is not for crazy people who do not have it all together.

Listen to counsel and receive instruction, that you may be wise in your latter days.
Proverbs 19:20 NKJV

Counsel is for wise people and those seeking to be wise, especially in the latter part of life. Counselors help you sift through your thoughts, discover patterns in behavior, pull out necessary priorities to obtain what you are looking for, and help resolve questions and issues in your relationships. They can take an objective approach and give recommendations based on wisdom and knowledge that they have gained through research and practice. We do ourselves a disservice running from such an invaluable resource.

    Not all these resources may be readily accessible for you but seek them all out throughout your life. Life happens, so each of these may have to be reassigned over time, but that is expected. Pray and seek a new source, just don't attempt to do without for too long.

Pray with me:

Dear God, I seek your overall protection for my spouse and me. Protect our minds against the accusations of the devil. Protect our hearts that malice, hate, envy nor jealousy would take root. Defend us, one to another, when society and comparison attempt to devalue who we are for another. Cover us with your grace in the midst of imperfections and opportunities to continue to grow. Give us the eyes to see where and when to flee from imposing danger. Encamp your angels around us so that no harm, mentally, physically or spiritually may prevail against us. In Jesus' name I pray. Amen.

Declaration

I am the guardian of my relationship. I stand in bold conviction to attack, defend, cover and flee consistently as much as needed to keep my relationship healthy. I acknowledge that my spouse and I are on the same team. The enemy is not within but without. We will not let Satan, the world or our own flesh to triumphantly deceive or misdirect our union. I will not protect passively but intentionally and aggressively. No weapon formed against us will prosper. We are mighty in the land. Our marriage is built upon the rock of our faith in God and the gates of hell shall not prevail against it. I will tear down my own pride before I let my pride tear down our marriage. My spouse and my relationship are valuable to me, and my actions will give evidence of this.

Chapter 12:

Love Always Trusts

Chapter 12
LOVE ALWAYS TRUSTS

For whatever reason, so many believe you can have a successful relationship without trust. Of course, they want to be able to trust, but trusting makes them feel vulnerable and foolish. It is but only a feeling of foolishness, however. It is foolish to believe you could navigate through a relationship without trust. With so much pessimism and vocal platforms for those who have been betrayed and have become bitter, a fear resonates that causes us to feel gullible when we put faith in the success of our relationships.

What questions play in your head that challenges you to believe in the success of your relationship?

_____

_____

_____

_____

_____

_____

One of the reasons we don't trust is because we have wrongfully partnered trust with the idea that the one we trust will never let us down, never hurt us and never disappoint us. That is just far from the reality, not because we have ill intentions but simply because we are imperfect. Trust acknowledges these things and moves beyond them to say that I trust that we will navigate through the hurt and disappointment. Therefore, I do not need a plan A or B, just a true, authentic commitment. Love will remain committed to the other person, but if the relationship is primarily built on selfish desire to draw someone close to you, you will never establish the needed trust in the union.

Chapter 12

What is It Anyway?

If trust isn't believing that someone will not hurt you, then, what is it? Of course, trust means the reliance on the integrity of another, but I would like to add is that trust simply relinquishes you from the need to know. We often do so much to prepare ourselves for failure and let down. When we put so much energy to prepare for let downs and setbacks, we cannot develop trust in the process. Just think how you would walk if you thought every step you took could cause you to trip over or sink into the earth. You'd question every step and take a longer time to make them. How much can we accomplish in our relationships with that same mindset?

Activity

Nothing to Fear but Fear Itself

Catalog those things that you fear happening in your relationship, even if you do not believe your spouse would cause you to experience those things. Ask your spouse if they would be willing to share out their fears as well. Pray and cover each other in managing these fears. Write yours below.

_____

_____

_____

_____

_____

_____

Grass Roots

You may be putting the pressure on your mate to give you a reason to trust them; however, the greater root to your lack of trust is that of a lack of trust in God. Now, it doesn't mean that we ought not be aware of apparent concerns in our relationships. It means that refraining from doing things God asks us to do in our relationship is a lack of trust that, in the presence of our view of our relationships, we believe we can and should do as He has instructed. Where God may instruct us to do more or to turn the cheek, we do not trust God's instruction to be sound. If we did, even if it was difficult, we would still acknowledge that we should do those things rather than come up with reasons not to do something. Let's be honest. We have all been there. In fact, doing it God's way can sometimes involve a period where you question your sanity because the fruit of your labor doesn't always come instantly.

I am going to record some scriptures below that can be difficult to commit to. For each, write down any reservations you have and take them to God and your spouse. Pray over them and commit to applying the instructions through your trust in God's sound wisdom.

Then Peter came to Him and asked, "Lord, how many times will my brother sin against me and I forgive him and let it go? Up to seven times? Jesus answered him, "I say to you, not up to seven times, but seventy times seven." ~ Matthew 19:21-22

_____

_____

_____

_____

Bless and show kindness to those who curse you, pray for those that mistreat you. Whoever strikes you on the cheek, offer him the other one also [simply ignore insignificant insults or losses and do not bother to retaliate – maintain your dignity]. Whoever takes away your coat, do not withhold your shirt from him either. ~ Luke 6:28-29

_____

_____

_____

Chapter 12

But to the married [believers] I give instructions – not I, but the Lord – that the wife is not to separate from her husband, (but even if she does leave him, let her remain single or else be reconciled to her husband) and that the husband should not leave his wife.
~ I Corinthians 7:10

_____

_____

_____

The husband must fulfill his [marital] duty to his wife [with good will and kindness], and likewise the wife to her husband. The wife does not have [exclusive] authority over her own body, but the husband shares with her; and likewise the husband does not have [exclusive] authority over his body, but the wife shares with him. Do not deprive each other [of marital rights], except perhaps by mutual consent for a time, so that you may devote yourselves [unhindered] to prayer but come together again so that Satan will not tempt you [to sin] because of your lack of self-control. ~ I Corinthians 7:3-5

_____

_____

_____

_____

These are just a few scriptures that can be hard to follow, especially when challenges present themselves in our relationships. Keep in mind, God reminds us that His word will never return to Him without completing what it set out to do (Isaiah 55:11). When we follow God's commandments and instructions, we leave the responsibility of the fruit that is produced and the outcome in His hands, but if we elect to do it our own way, we must assume full responsibility for the fruit and outcome. We must ask ourselves if we trust ourselves more than we trust God. Are we more responsible than God?

Trusting Idols

Sometimes it is not a lack of trust in God that is the challenge. Sometimes it is the excessive trust in something else that gets in the way of following what God tells us to do. These things do not have to be considered bad things, but our trust in them over God becomes a problem. Some of us trust in our jobs for our finances more than we trust in God, so conversations over tithing or making family changes can be difficult. Some of us trust in our parents' advice more, even if it disagrees with what God says. Of course, it is likely that our parents mean well, but it doesn't mean they will always offer the best of advice. Some of us put more trust in our own way of thinking than that of God. If it doesn't make sense in our heads, we will not follow God even though He told us not to rely on our own understanding (Proverbs 3:5-6).

What are some things you trust or rely on that sometimes get in the way of receiving God's instruction for your life?

_____

_____

_____

_____

_____

"When you cry out [for help], let your [ridiculous] collection of idols save you. But the wind will carry them all away, a [mere] breath will take them. But he who takes refuge in Me will possess the land [Judea] and will inherit My holy mountain." ~ Isaiah 57:13

Remember, every idol that we hold in our hearts will be exposed for their lack in comparison to God. We are better off proactively turning away from them and trusting God.

Chapter 12

The Benefits

There are some invaluable benefits to trusting God at His word and being willing to walk in His way and follow His commandments. Put a check in each box that is valuable to you. Discover the benefits you desire from trusting God.

☐ **Greater efficiency for reaching relational and personal goals.** Proverbs 3:5 states that He would make our crooked places straight.

☐ **Safety.** In Proverbs 29:25, God promises that those who trust in Him will be kept safe.

☐ **Strength for challenges and opportunities.** Isaiah 12:2 declares that those who trust in the Lord will find strength for their battles.

☐ **Defense.** Isaiah 12:2 also declares that those who trust in the Lord will be defended by Him concerning their battles.

☐ **Enjoyment.** Though there will be hardships in life, I Timothy 6:17 declares that those who trust in God will be provided everything for their enjoyment.

☐ **Fortification and endurance.** Psalms 125:1 declares that those who trust in God will not be shaken and will be able to endure forever.

☐ **Life after death.** Even when things seem dead or hopeless, those who trust in God know and experience things being brought back to life, according to II Corinthians 9:10.

☐ **An escape when we are troubled.** Even through the discourse of our imperfections, when we should perish in the presence of our vulnerabilities, in Jeremiah 39:18, God promises that we will not perish but escape.

I would be surprised if you did not check every box. I know I did. All these things are a great benefit to my life and my relationship. The reality is that without trust, we will hit a wall in our relationships; however, with trust, we will be able to walk through walls.

Fear Factor

Before we close the activities in this chapter. It is important to revisit fear, which is perhaps the biggest nemesis of trust. The difference between fear and trust dictates the persona of our lives. People who live in fear try to avoid suffering, but people who trust will believe that they can overcome suffering. In every aspect of life, everything meaningful, has a season of suffering. There is a period of nine months of pregnancy to produce a beautiful baby (not to mention potentially hours of active labor). There are twelve years of schooling to produce a diploma, and four to eight years to produce bachelor's and master's degrees. Every great workout session causes us to exert energy beyond our norms, and it takes a season of it to produce a healthy lifestyle, along with the discipline of good dieting. The bible speaks of suffering being used so that we lack nothing (James 1:4), yet we put so much effort into avoiding it. I hope we begin to realize that fear is a greater danger than suffering itself.

The fear of man will prove to be a snare, but whoever trusts in the Lord will be kept safe.
~Proverbs 29:25

On the show *Fear Factor*, contestants are challenged to complete obstacles that could possibly insight fear. The reality is that the contestants are never actually in any real danger (not to say that the obstacles do not appear dangerous or challenging). It would be a liability if the show ever actually did not have the appropriate safeguards in place to keep the contestants from becoming seriously injured. However, if the contestant is overcome with fear, he/she will elect to bail out of the contest. In the same way, fear immobilizes us and our relationships. God has the appropriate safeguards in place when we follow Him, but fear makes us bail out, removing us from the ability to "win the prize" in life.

Since fear desires to ensnare, attack and overcome us. We are going to take the attack to fear itself. Below, I want you to write down a fear you have when it comes to your own self-preservation or that of your relationship. For every fear you list, I want you to write a *trust statement* to protest the fear. Remember the promises of trusting God. For example, if I fear communicating concerns to my wife will just cause arguments and ultimate separation, I can remember that God fulfills all our enjoyment and that He fortifies us so that we will not be shaken; therefore, I trust that continuing to

Chapter 12

communicate concerns and lovingly resolve problems will continue to strengthen and affirm my relationship. Now, you give it a go.

Fear: _____
_____

Trust statement: _____
_____

Fear: _____
_____

Trust statement: _____
_____

Fear: _____
_____

Trust statement: _____
_____

Remember, fear enslaves you. Trust in God empowers you.

Pray with me:

Heavenly Father, I trust you with my whole heart. Though life produces many challenges and obstacles, I know that You will not only keep me safe through it all, but You will allow me to prosper. When fear attempts to cast a shadow on my life, I will look to You to be my light and refuge. Thank you for desiring to do well in my life. Help me to cast down any idol that attempts to stand above You. You are the ultimate source of everything that I have and everything that is promised for me and my relationship. Thank you. In Jesus' name I pray. Amen.

Declaration

I will not be governed by fear. I am safe. All my needs are being provided. All my desires are being shaped. I will trust in the Lord in every season. My faith and hope in Him will guide my choices and actions. I do not desire that my spouse is perfect. Instead, I operate in the trust that God will lead us through our imperfections and sufferings. We are being made stronger and more resilient. I believe in the future of my relationship, because I trust that God is for us and not against us. He has established the proper safeguards to guide us through every season of our lives.

Chapter 13:

Love Always Hopes

Chapter 13
LOVE ALWAYS HOPES

Have you ever participated in a tug-o-war game? Perhaps, you have at least seen one. Sometimes, there is a ribbon tied at the center of a rope, and two teams pull from opposing sides. The goal then would be to get the ribbon to cross a designated threshold to win the match. A more exciting version of the game is when the teams compete to attempt to pull the other team into the impeding mud bath in between them. A good team will plant their heels firmly into the ground to offer a strong resistance to the other team's pull. Then, keeping the core of their bodies tight, they use their upper body strength to pull the rope towards them.

The battle between hope and doubt is like a game of tug-o-war. Each one fights for our sense of being. Hope pulls us to believe, to be excited about our futures and to hold on to our goals and the promises of God. Doubt pulls us to play it safe with expectation, to acknowledge the opposition, and to give up on things we desire in life. If either side gets our mind to reach a certain threshold, it will govern our attitudes and actions. Whichever one that has the stronger foundation in our minds usually has the advantage over the other. In the most critical of situations, the battles forges until one absolutely dominates the other, leaving that side figuratively in the mud, suffering a devastating defeat. When doubt wins in this way, usually it will epitomize our greatest sense of failure and pessimism. When hope prevails, it is a doorway to a new, exciting life!

It's Time to Play the Game

In a moment, I want you to process what drives your perspectives towards life, you and your relationship. What philosophies in life do you live by that give you hope despite obstacles? What philosophies in life do you live by that cause you to doubt the realization of great and desirable outcomes? What things have you witnessed in life that motivate you to maintain hope? What things have you witnessed that have made you doubtful?

Chapter 13

TUG-O-WAR

Things that make you hopeful	Things that make you doubtful
Ex: Many people in my life have experienced success, so I believe it is possible for me. *Ex: My pastor reminds us that God has the final say.*	*Ex: I see everybody else around me achieving goals, but I just can't seem to achieve my own.* *Ex: My mom would always tell me to keep my head out of the clouds. Life is simply what we have now.*

If your list of your doubtfulness is longer than the list of your hopefulness, do not fret just yet. Not every thought, memory or philosophy carries the same weight. For that reason, I want you to rate the importance or effect of each thing on a scale of 1 to 5; 1 being not much affect at all, and 5 being something you pretty much live by day-to-day. Once you have rated each, add up each side and write the totals below.

Hopefulness: _____

Doubtfulness: _____

It is important to know what mindset we have been dominated by in our lives. Hopefully (no pun intended), none of us are willing to stay in an unwanted mindset. I hope none of us desire to live a doubtful life. For that reason, I would like to offer you an opportunity to add something to your hopefulness list that you can rank at 100 points, so that (unless you wrote twenty things down in your doubtfulness list and rated them all with 5's) you can begin to live a hopeful life.

God is the God over the impossible. In Him, against all hope, we can still have hope. One yes from Him will overcome a million no's. God can not only keep you from death. He can raise you from death. If you assign to who God truly is, you can always find hope during whatever circumstance you may face.

How to Remain in Hope

If you are like most people, it may not be impossible to have hope. When you hear a great sermon or watch an inspiring movie, you may feel a sense of hope coming upon you. However, the challenge is remaining in hope. Usually, over time, we witness the energy created in the initial moment of inspiration begin to lose its impact. The reason is that there is a difference in feeling hopeful and having a resolve to hope. A resolve to hope will remain in hope, but how is that possible?

As we discussed in the book, David would often find himself beginning to doubt and worry. The reality is that he faced real and huge challenges throughout the course of his life. However, he can be counted as having a resolve to hope because, though he

Chapter 13

acknowledged the adversity and his feelings, he would always turn to who God is to him.

Why, my soul, or you downcast? Why so disturbed within me? Put your hope in God, for I will yet praise him, my Savior and my God. ~ Psalms 42:5

David acknowledged who God is by praising Him. For those of us who have not done this before, it may seem crazy to believe that this act alone will ignite the hope from within, but the reality is that it is more than effective. In fact, the greater the burden, the greater the need to praise and the mightier the energy should be behind the praise. On one occasion, at the lowest of the low, I put on some worship music and sung and praised all by myself. At the beginning of the song, I felt defeated. Before the song was over, with tears in my eyes, I felt a strength in my spirit and a hope in my heart. I was committed to holding on to those things I was hopeful for.

Let's Go Crazy

Is it possible to feel like you are crazy while praising amid facing hell on earth? Absolutely. It is not the *logical* thing to do. But before you go off doubting the power of praise, I have an important assignment and activity for you. I want you to write down everything God currently is for you and everything you desire Him to be for you. After doing so, I want you to read your list out loud with conviction. Then, I want you to play a worship song (preferably one you know the lyrics to) and sing along. Don't worry. I can't sing either, but it still works. If you happen to not know the lyrics to any song, select one you are familiar with. If you are not familiar with any, tune in to a Christian music station on the radio or through an app or website. Basically, don't give yourself an excuse not to do this activity. Find a song that resonates with your spirit. Meditate on what you are believing and hoping for and praise God through the song.

Who is God to you?

_____

_____

_____

Alive in Famine

But the eyes of the Lord are on those whose hope is in His unfailing love, to deliver them from death and keep them alive in famine. ~Psalms 33:18

Some of the greatest challenges to maintaining hope is seeing a constancy of hardships or unwanted circumstances. If you are working for a company or within a field where there are a lot of people being laid off, you may begin to doubt that you will keep your job. If you find yourself arguing with your spouse often, you may begin to doubt that you will ever be on the same page. Considering how many marriages end in divorce, you may not believe that your marriage will survive the test of time. However, God does not ignore the famine around you, but states that those who will place their hope in Him will not perish in the famine.

Chapter 13

Therefore, it is okay to acknowledge the famine around you, but do not end that thought with a period. End it with a comma followed by "but God will keep me/us alive." For example, "Fifty percent of marriages are ending in divorce, but God will keep us together." What are some famine situations surrounding you and your relationships? Is it something that has been plaguing your family, generation to generation?

If you are going through real challenges, you do not have to ignore them. In fact, it is better to acknowledge them. Hope is not denial. Hope is seeing the challenge but also seeing victory and vindication beyond the challenge. I want to give you an opportunity to be hopeful, to recognize what challenges you are facing but put hope in God to deliver you from those challenges and grant you the desires of your heart. I want you to write down your challenges and those things that make you overall doubtful about life. This time, do not end them with a period. Place a comma after them and write a "but statement" that declares the power and promises of God are still in your favor.

Challenge or doubtful outlook: _____

_____,

But: _____

_____.

Challenge or doubtful outlook: _____

_____,

But: _____

_____.

Challenge or doubtful outlook: _____

_____,

But: _____

_____.

Challenge or doubtful outlook: _____

_____,

But: _____

_____.

On a regular basis, train your mind to include these "but statements" in your thought life. When you are seeing the obstacles, acknowledge the God above those obstacles and have hope.

Hope for Healing

One of the hardest things to hope for is reconciliation. Many marriages end under the *irreconcilable differences* clause. Most of the time, we get into these situations after burning out on unrealistic expectations for each other. It is to no surprise that many of us give up on the healing process because of unrealistic expectations of what the healing process should look like. Many of us believe that the process is linear meaning the relationship continues to improve day by day including the feelings, emotions and communication involved. The reality is usually we must dig deeper, thereby, usually causing more pain, disappointment and discomfort to get to the bottom of the complications in our relationships to then build something new and more affirmed. Seeing the relationship seemingly getting worse may cause us to become doubtful that we can ever enjoy our relationship.

There is a picture I've seen before. Two minors were digging for diamonds. One of them can be seen turning away just before the moment he reached the diamonds, while the other one was further off but still digging. Would the other one turn away, too? The first one did most of the work but did not receive the reward having lost hope just before the prize. How many relationships end just before the breakthrough, just before the epiphany that gives them the wisdom and resolve to love and thrive in their relationship? No matter if you are trying to right your wrongs or heal from being wronged, there is hope for your healing.

Chapter 13

    Two things happen in a healing process: the offended gets to mature in his/her ability to forgive and love unconditionally and the offender gets an opportunity to display a greater sense of discipline and commitment to do right by his/her mate. Usually, something specific challenges one person to offend the other. Over time, that person will endure those same temptations. With a strong conviction to reconcile, the offender can now fight the mindset that caused them to offend in the first place. This allows that person to not just plea to save the relationship but speak with greater confidence that the things that caused the pain will not prevail against the relationship again.

    The greatest opportunity in the healing process is the established assignments for both the offended and the offender. The offended usually never communicate what they need to heal: meaning what they need from the offender and what they need to do themselves to heal. The offender usually spends more time promising to "never do it again" rather than digging into the what drove his/her actions and getting the help and therapy to avoid repeating the behavior in the future. By establishing a plan, we give fuel for the hope that we can resolve the conflict.

Activity

The Assignment

For any area where you have been offended, write down what you need for your healing. If you absolutely do not know, counseling is a definite answer. If you have offended, write down what caused you to commit those acts (it is not the other person's fault you did something wrong). Dig deeper. Loneliness? Rejection? Pride? Write it out and develop a plan to overcome what drove you to hurt your loved one.

_____

_____

_____

_____

_____

_____

_____

Remember, hope is having expectant desire, not to have a reluctant wish. Believe in the promises of God. Believe that God can and will redeem you and your relationship. Believe that God can take you to a level in your own maturity and happiness in your relationship that you have never experienced before. Hope is not defining what you see; it is believing in what you have yet to see. Have hope in the unseen levels of your relationship.

Pray with me:

Dear God, I put my hope and my faith in You to accomplish things only Your sovereign power and glory could accomplish. Hoping in you will never put me to shame. I am thankful for that promise. I pray You give me the strength, joy and peace placing hope in You brings. Thank you for building me up through adversity and the delay of Your promises. Thank you for seeing those things I need outside of my desires and working on the total person. I am better because of Your guidance and discipline. Help me to keep hope in my capabilities, the value of my spouse, and the success of our relationship. In Jesus' name I pray. Amen.

Declaration

I see my relationship beyond the past limitations and the current obstacles. I have hope in our future. My mate and I are both becoming better people, better lovers and stronger hearts. Regardless of whatever we face, there is a stronger God I serve that can deliver us from it. I have hope in the victory and the vindication promised by God. I have hope that we can travel to the deepest of our pains and rise to the greatest sense of love, peace and fulfillment. I have an even greater hope that our example will be a light that inspires and motivates others.

Chapter 14:

Love Always Perseveres

Chapter 14
LOVE ALWAYS PERSEVERES

Why do we give up? We have so many desires and goals, but we give up. How do we become convinced that things will never work out? One thing is true, which is why *What Is Love* was written. If we are not willing to do the things the right way, we will burn out on doing things the wrong way, unless we finally decide to yield to how we are designed to love. The other part of giving up, which is what I believe most couples experience, is that we lean on how discouraged our flesh is in being unfulfilled. Some of you may not appreciate me connecting unfulfilled desires to our flesh rather than our spirit, but what I have discovered is that our spirits are filled by what we are able to contribute to others. This means that, while desiring to be pursued and loved on, I can spiritually find fulfillment and treasures in the fruits of serving my spouse. I know this from experience. The other part is that, even amidst struggles, the spirit may struggle but would never desire to quit or get a divorce. It simply goes against the Spirit's desire to do right by God. As Jesus once said, "the spirit is willing, but the body is weak" (Matthew 26:41).

The reality is that our minds respond one way to trials and unmet needs and our spirits respond another. Our brains are fueled by our feelings, where as our spirits are fueled by the Word of God. If we receive undesirable outcomes, our brains instruct us to remove ourselves from the environment because we do not feel good about it. However, our spirits are willing to do what God instructs us to do regardless of how it makes us feel.

Chapter 14

Activity

I Got a Feeling

Write down things that are being fueled by your emotions. Answer this question: Where have you intentionally made the decision to do what you want to do, contrary to what you believe God instructed you to do? In these areas, pray to relinquish the driving force away from the emotions and feelings that have driven your choices and give them over to spiritual discipline. Determine what directed you to knowingly do something differently than what you were spiritually led to do and repent (turn away from) concerning that reason.

_____
_____
_____
_____
_____
_____
_____
_____
_____
_____
_____

Pain Killers

One of my good friends is on her journey of health and wellness. She has gained the capacity to push herself in the gym. On one occasion, she pushed herself a little too far and strained her back to the point she couldn't work out for a while. After a doctor's visit, she was given some medicine to kill or numb the pain. After a while, she returned to working out only to find her back strained again without even over-exerting herself. Surely enough, more pain medicine was prescribed. You wouldn't believe it, but it even happened a third time. Finally, her and husband decided to take a deeper look into the situation and heal the area of her back instead of settling for medication that only killed the pain.

If we are honest with ourselves, when we experience pain in our relationships, our immediate source or medicine is turning to something that will numb the pain: alcohol, distance, masturbation, infidelity, or simply ending the relationship to end the problem. However, just as it is with the pain killers my friend took, none of these things allow us to really get back on our feet. If we never take a deeper look into what is causing the pain, we never are truly healed, and the moment something reignites those injuries, we are bedridden all over again.

New Prescription

What are some areas of pain in yourself or in your relationship? You may even want to include pain from older relationships if you were never healed from them. What are you using to cope with these pains? If it is only treating the pain but producing no healing, seek help in these areas through prayer, counseling, and accountability. If you haven't already, share these areas with your spouse and solicit his/her help and support, even if they are a part of the pain. Give them an opportunity to rectify the situation.

Area of pain: _____

_____

_____

What was used to numb the pain: _____

_____

_____

Chapter 14

What is the new prescription: _____

_____

Area of pain: _____

_____

_____

What was used to numb the pain: _____

_____

_____

What is the new prescription: _____

_____

Area of pain: _____

_____

_____

What was used to numb the pain: _____

_____

_____

What is the new prescription: _____

_____

_____

Purpose Over Pain

Anyone that has ever been out-of-shape and worked to get into shape knows that there is a pain associated with the process. Again, mothers know that child labor isn't a pleasant experience. What enables both groups to persevere is that there is a purpose greater than the pain. The pain is not desirable, but they are willing to go through it for the goal on the other side of that pain. The challenge for most relationships is that we unite through desire and passion but never establish a purpose other than to fulfill those desires and passions. The goal is not strong enough to persevere through the pain and discomfort of some of the seasons we will experience.

How have you defined the purpose of your relationship? Why did you get together? Is it a strong enough reason to stay together? Does the difficulty you are facing nullify your purpose or is it a barrier that needs to be overcome? Does overcoming the barrier strengthen your ability to accomplish your purpose? We rarely consciously process the answers to these questions. Usually, the difficulties take our minds completely off the focus of purpose. Obviously, it is even more dangerous when we never focused on purpose to begin with.

Chapter 14

> **Activity**
>
> *Purpose Defined*
>
> If you have never consciously determined the purpose in your relationship, I want to give you an opportunity to do so now. If you already have one, great! Consider how important that purpose is to you. If it isn't that important, meditate to see if you can discover a "higher calling" for your marriage. A purpose may be to break generational curses or trends. It may be to build and maintain a strong foundation for your children and provide an example. If it is important to you and beyond materialism, it can be a purpose.
>
> _____
> _____
> _____
> _____
> _____
> _____
> _____

Most people may not realize their purposes initially. Sometimes, the understanding of these purposes begins to evolve over time. It may be the business you end up starting together or the foundation you create. You may discover that the differences between your personalities and skillsets are just what the two of you need to both become successful. The bible speaks of one putting to flight 1,000 but two together putting to flight ten thousand (Joshua 23:10).

Also, the very pains we experience ultimately shape our personal purpose. As we mature, purpose matures. Your reason for getting together in your relationship will not always be your purpose in the relationship. Keep this in mind. Is there any form of true success that comes without difficulty? If not, are difficulties to blame for absolute failure or is our response to those difficulties to be blamed?

For the Children

I wanted to briefly address an available mindset that parades around our society. There are many people who believe you should not stay married just because you have children. They believe that if you are not happy, then the children will not be happy either. They share the standpoint that, as a mother or as a father, they do not want to teach their children to just deal with things you do not deserve to go through. I totally understand where they are coming from with these views. I, too, do not believe that you should be willing to just sit and suffer through a relationship.

However, it is proven that there is a high chance that our children suffer greatly at the "violent dismembering of the 'one flesh' of marriage" (Malachi 2:16). This is possibly one of the reasons why God hates divorce. In almost every category of undesired behavior of children, from school dropout rates to becoming serial killers, there is a strong correlation with having been raised in a single-parent (fatherless) home. Even in your "freedom" from the problems of your marriage, most children go well into adulthood without fully healing from divorce. Even though you may have shown them to not tolerate mistreatment, they also never see an example of how to be good husbands and wives, so their marriages usually end in divorce as well. They never witness how to work through relational challenges. We cannot deny this impact.

Now, I, too, still agree that the answer isn't to simply stay and suffer in a relationship. Hopefully, this information creates enough purpose for us to dig in and really resolve the difficulties so that we can begin to thrive in our marriages. We will then enjoy our relationships and our children can maintain a sense of security and well-being accompanied with an example of how to prevail through the obstacles they will face in their own future relationships. If this isn't important enough for you, and you currently do not have children, I respectfully ask you to consider never having them.

Chapter 14

Again, the spiritual, emotional and psychological implications of divorce are too volatile to gamble with the lives of children who have no choice in the situation.

Pray with me:

Heavenly Father, I believe that nothing is over until You say it is over. With You, what is valuable to me always has a fighting chance. You have placed great value in the covenant of marriage and I will not take it lightly or give up on it so easily. Please, guide me and navigate me through the challenges that we will face. Show us how to see the light through the darkness. Help us to live in purpose by revealing those purposes to us. Thank you for entrusting us as walking, breathing examples of people who trust You and place their hope in You. That is purpose. In Jesus' name I pray. Amen.

Declaration

I am not a quitter. God has gifted me with the ability to endure, to see through pain and live in purpose. I do not need life to be easy to be successful. I realize I am strong through Christ who strengthens me. I will not give up on goals and dreams. I will press through patiently and will consistently see light through the trials of life and my relationship. I will prevail. We will prevail. Failure is not an option.

Outro:

Love Never Fails

Outro
LOVE NEVER FAILS

As stated in my initial letter to you, I hope you have benefited from taking this journey through the workbook. It is not a brief workbook, so I hope that you did not race through the process. I like that it is called a workbook because if we want to be successful in our relationships, we must do the work. I hope you have been intentional and are seeing the fruit of your committed process. I hope you will revisit many of your responses to discover how and where you and your relationship are shifting. Just as important as promoting the health of our relationships, there is a great need to simply focus on learning and improving ourselves. I want you to take a moment to journal what you have learned about yourself and how you believe you are becoming a better person and spouse.

_____
_____
_____
_____
_____
_____
_____
_____
_____
_____

Throughout the book and the workbook, we have touched on some sensitive topics. Possibly, many of our opportunities and faults have been exposed. The intent of this book wasn't for any of you to conclude that you are a lousy lover (however, if it is true then simply do something about it). The hope is that you recognize that there is just so much untapped territory for love to dwell in our hearts and our disciplines. Is it sound to give up before love has an opportunity to mature within us? Unless he/she is a baby genius, it would be unwise to give a three-year old a calculus test and expect them to pass. As romanticized as love is made out to be, it is not something that we can just dive into an expect to be successful right at the start. We must be intentional and studious.

Love does not fail, but we simply fail to allow love to fully evolve inside of us and within our relationships. We can never lose with love. We can never lose by doing what is right. On the other side, the benefits of doing what is wrong will never last and will never prevail. I have personally, deeply struggled within my own marriage, but I would not have the sense of strength, resilience, resolve and conviction without those struggles. Today, I am more of who I desired to be for my wife on our wedding day, but first I had to discover where I had the opportunities to become better: the things I lacked and the things I possessed that stood in the way. Life and experiences had to reveal those things.

The bible speaks of love drawing us to get to know the person in the mirror, more and more (I Corinthians 13:8-13). Otherwise, our identities are an enigma, even unto ourselves. If you gained great revelation through this journey, don't fight it. Do not deny it. You will not profit from pride, fear or any other thing that will cause you to fight off becoming better and doing what is honorable to God and the people you value. Many others have responded by becoming bitter, harsh, resentful and selfish without realizing they have only promised themselves internal suffering until they release that mentality.

Realize this, nobody desires better for you than God! He will not ask you to do anything that brings your value down. He only desires to reveal the worth, strength, power, confidence and ability He, Himself, has gifted you with. You give wood to a carpenter expecting him to make something great and useful out of it. You give an investor money anticipating she will be able to grow the value of what was given. God gives us life expecting we create something useful and great out of it, increasing the investment He has made in us. Yes, while writing this workbook, my own marriage went through tests and challenges, but at its conclusion, I am madly in love with my wife and I am gaining more and more opportunities to express it. Intimacy and communication are growing. We are taking steps forward. Where I may have doubted before, I am more convinced that I am married to the most phenomenal woman in the world. I am blessed. I am grateful. I am hopeful, and… I feel good. Where I once felt a sense of discouragement in myself and in my marriage, I am excited about the possibilities that are ahead of us. If I told you what all that took place in between the beginning of writing this book and this moment, you might have chosen to run in the opposite direction, but the opposite direction was not where I'd find what we have now and what we will have in the future. Again, love never fails. It will never let you down. It will only make life better for us.

Pray with me:

Heavenly Father, continue to discipline me to love. You have provided a great example by loving me through everything: the good, the bad and the ugly. I acknowledge that I cannot be successful on this journey without walking with You and being directed by You. You have promised victory. I desire to hold on to that promise. I have been imperfect in my pursuits, but I am so grateful for Your grace, mercy, patience and unconditional love towards me. Since You have not given up on me, I have no reason to give up on myself. I can and will be who You created me to be – a person who loves. In Jesus' name I pray. Amen.

Declaration

Love never fails. I will never be a failure in love. I am committed to becoming the best version of myself, for myself, for my spouse, for my children, and for anyone who needs an example of how to trust God through everything. The fruit of my marriage will be beyond what I initially anticipated on our wedding day. Our best years and moments are still ahead of us. God is not done fulfilling His promises and blessings. I will serve God with my life. I will serve God through unconditionally loving my spouse. We will not be easily broken. We will not fail. We will prevail.

Made in the USA
Columbia, SC
29 October 2024